2ⁿᵈ EDITION

Ventures 4

STUDENT'S BOOK

Gretchen Bitterlin   Dennis Johnson   Donna Price   Sylvia Ramirez

K. Lynn Savage (Series Editor)

CAMBRIDGE
UNIVERSITY PRESS

CAMBRIDGE UNIVERSITY PRESS
Cambridge, New York, Melbourne, Madrid, Cape Town,
Singapore, São Paulo, Delhi, Mexico City

Cambridge University Press
32 Avenue of the Americas, New York, NY 10013-2473, USA

www.cambridge.org
Information on this title: www.cambridge.org/9781107681576

First published 2008

Printed in Mexico by Quad / Graphics Querétaro, S.A. de C.V.

A catalog record for this publication is available from the British Library.

ISBN 978-1-107-68157-6 Student's Book with Audio CD
ISBN 978-1-107-66194-3 Workbook with Audio CD
ISBN 978-1-139-88349-8 Online Workbook
ISBN 978-1-107-69841-3 Teacher's Edition with Assessment Audio CD / CD-ROM
ISBN 978-1-107-63513-5 Class Audio CDs
ISBN 978-1-107-61945-6 Presentation Plus

Additional resources for this publication at www.cambridge.org/ventures

Art direction, book design, photo research, and layout services: Q2A / Bill Smith
Audio production: CityVox, LLC

Authors' acknowledgments

The authors would like to acknowledge and thank focus group participants and reviewers for their insightful comments, as well as Cambridge University Press editorial, marketing, and production staffs, whose thorough research and attention to detail have resulted in a quality product.

The publishers would also like to extend their particular thanks to the following reviewers and consultants for their valuable insights and suggestions:

Kit Bell, LAUSD division of Adult and Career Education, Los Angeles, CA; **Bethany Bogage**, San Diego Community College District, San Diego, CA; **Leslie Keaton Boyd**, Dallas ISD, Dallas, TX; **Barbara Brodsky**, Teaching Work Readiness English for Refugees – Lutheran Family Services, Omaha, NE; **Jessica Buchsbaum**, City College of San Francisco, San Francisco, CA; **Helen Butner**, University of the Fraser Valley, British Columbia, Canada; **Sharon Churchill Roe**, Acadia University, Wolfville, NS, Canada; **Lisa Dolehide**, San Mateo Adult School, San Mateo, CA; **Yadira M. Dominguez**, Dallas ISD, Dallas, TX; **Donna M. Douglas**, College of DuPage, Glen Ellyn, IL; **Latarsha Dykes**, Broward Collge, Pembroke Pines, FL; **Megan L. Ernst**, Glendale Community College, Glendale, CA; **Megan Esler**, Portland Community College, Portland, OR; **Jennifer Fadden**, Fairfax County Public Schools, Fairfax, VA; **Fotine Fahouris**, College of Marin, Kentfield, CA; **Lynn Francis, M.A, M.S.**, San Diego Community College, San Diego, CA; **Danielle Gines**, Tarrant County College, Arlington, TX; **Katherine Hayne**, College of Marin, Kentfield, CA; **Armenuhi Hovhannes**, City College of San Francisco, San Francisco, CA; **Fayne B. Johnson**; **Martha L. Koranda**, College of DuPage, Glen Ellyn, IL; **Daphne Lagios**, San Mateo Adult School, San Mateo, CA; **Judy Langelier**, School District of Palm Beach County, Wellington, FL; **Janet Les**, Chilliwack Community Services, Chilliwack, British Columbia, Canada; **Keila Louzada**, Northern Virginia Community College, Sterling, VA; **Karen Mauer**, Fort Worth ISD, Fort Worth, TX; **Silvana Mehner**, Northern Virginia Community College, Sterling, VA; **Astrid T. Mendez-Gines,** Tarrant County College, Arlington, TX; **Beverly A. Miller**, Houston Community College, Houston, TX; **José Montes, MS. Ed.**, The English Center, Miami-Dade County Public Schools, Miami, FL; **Suzi Monti**, Community College of Baltimore County, Baltimore, MD; **Irina Morgunova**, Roxbury Community College, Roxbury Crossing, MA; **Julia Morgunova**, Roxbury Community College, Roxbury Crossing, MA; **Susan Otero**, Fairfax County Public Schools, Fairfax, VA; **Sergei Paromchik**, Hillsborough County Public Schools, Tampa, FL; **Pearl W. Pigott**, Houston Community College, Houston, TX; **Marlene Ramirez**, The English Center, Miami-Dade County Public Schools, Miami, FL; **Cory Rayala**, Harbor Service Center, LAUSD, Los Angeles, CA; **Catherine M. Rifkin**, Florida State College at Jacksonville, Jacksonville, FL; **Danette Roe**, Evans Community Adult School, Los Angeles, CA; **Maria Roy**, Kilgore College, Kilgore, TX; **Jill Shalongo**, Glendale Community College, Glendale, CA, and Sierra Linda High School, Phoenix, AZ; **Laurel Owensby Slater**, San Diego Community College District, San Diego, CA; **Rheba Smith**, San Diego Community College District, San Diego, CA; **Jennifer Snyder**, Portland Community College, Portland, OR; **Mary K. Solberg**, Metropolitan Community College, Omaha, NE; **Rosanne Vitola**, Austin Community College, Austin, TX

Scope and sequence

UNIT TITLE TOPIC	FUNCTIONS	LISTENING AND SPEAKING	VOCABULARY	GRAMMAR FOCUS
Welcome pages 2–5	▪ Exchanging information ▪ Discussing study habits and strategies	▪ Listening to people talk about study habits and strategies ▪ Asking about study habits and strategies ▪ Talking about classmates' study habits and strategies	▪ Study habits and strategies	▪ Contrasting psst continuous and simple past ▪ Contrasting simple past and present perfect
Unit 1 **Personal information** pages 6–17 Topic: **Ways to be smart**	▪ Describing personal strengths ▪ Expressing opinions ▪ Expressing agreement and disagreement	▪ Asking about aptitudes ▪ Discussing multiple intelligences ▪ Giving opinions	▪ Adjectives and adverbs ▪ Multiple intelligences ▪ Prefixes and roots	▪ Nouns, verbs, adjectives, and adverbs ▪ Noun clauses with *that* ▪ *so* and *that*
Unit 2 **At school** pages 18–29 Topic: **Planning for success**	▪ Inquiring about educational opportunities ▪ Describing educational goals ▪ Describing successful people	▪ Asking about courses and classes ▪ Discussing how to continue one's education ▪ Discussing obstacles and successes	▪ Education and careers ▪ Educational requirements	▪ The present passive ▪ Infinitives after the passive ▪ *be + supposed to* and *be + not supposed to*
Review: Units 1 and 2 pages 30–31		▪ Understanding a conversation		
Unit 3 **Friends and family** pages 32–43 Topic: **Parents and children**	▪ Discussing appropriate behaviors at home and school ▪ Using polite forms of language	▪ Asking about rules at home and at school ▪ Asking questions indirectly ▪ Talking about past events and experiences	▪ Rules and expectations ▪ Word families	▪ Indirect *Wh-* questions ▪ Indirect *Yes / No* questions ▪ *say* and *tell* with reported speech
Unit 4 **Health** pages 44–55 Topic: **Stressful situations**	▪ Discussing stress ▪ Expressing necessity and lack of necessity ▪ Making suggestions ▪ Expressing past regrets	▪ Asking about stress ▪ Discussing ways to cope with stress ▪ Giving advice about past actions	▪ Stress and ways to cope ▪ Suffixes	▪ *should, shouldn't, have to, don't have to* ▪ *should have* and *shouldn't have* ▪ *must* and *may / might*
Review: Units 3 and 4 pages 56–57		▪ Understanding a phone conversation		
Unit 5 **Around town** pages 58–69 Topic: **Community involvement**	▪ Describing volunteer responsibilities ▪ Describing a sequence of events ▪ Describing repeated actions in the past and present	▪ Asking about volunteer activities ▪ Discussing personal experiences of volunteering or helping people ▪ Discussing schedules	▪ Volunteerism ▪ Words with positive and negative meanings	▪ Clauses with *until* and *as soon as* ▪ Repeated actions in the present and past ▪ Contrasting *used to* and *be used to*

READING	WRITING	LIFE SKILLS	PRONUNCIATION
■ Reading a paragraph about bad weather	■ Writing sentences about your partner	■ Discussing study habits and strategies for learning English	■ Pronouncing key vocabulary
■ Reading an article about multiple intelligences ■ Skimming to predict what a reading is about	■ Writing a descriptive paragraph about a primary intelligence ■ Using a topic sentence and supporting details	■ Using a dictionary ■ Reading and understanding a visual diagram	■ Pronouncing key vocabulary
■ Reading an article about an immigrant family ■ Scanning to find specific information	■ Writing a descriptive paragraph about a successful person ■ Using specific details such as facts, examples, and reasons	■ Using a dictionary or thesaurus to identify synonyms ■ Reading and understanding a chart about the location of vocational classes	■ Pronouncing key vocabulary
			■ *-ed* verb endings
■ Reading an article about barriers between generations ■ Noticing words that repeat to get an idea of what a reading is about	■ Writing an expository paragraph about a difference between generations ■ Using a transition within a paragraph	■ Using a dictionary ■ Reading and understanding a chart ■ Interpreting census bureau information	■ Pronouncing key vocabulary
■ Reading an article about stress ■ Relating the title and section heads to personal experience	■ Writing a descriptive paragraph about how to cope with stress ■ Using causes and effects to organize a paragraph	■ Reading and understanding a bar graph ■ Discussing stress in the workplace	■ Pronouncing key vocabulary
			■ Contrasting intonation of direct and indirect *Wh-* questions
■ Reading an article about volunteers ■ Using context clues to guess if the meaning of a word is positive or negative	■ Writing a descriptive paragraph about someone who made a difference ■ Making writing more interesting by including details that answer *Wh-* questions	■ Reading and understanding ads for volunteer positions ■ Discussing volunteer activities	■ Pronouncing key vocabulary

UNIT TITLE TOPIC	FUNCTIONS	LISTENING AND SPEAKING	VOCABULARY	GRAMMAR FOCUS
Unit 6 **Time** pages 70–81 Topic: **Time and technology**	• Expressing agreement and disagreement • Giving opinions and reasons	• Talking about time-saving devices • Discussing the advantages and disadvantages of technology	• Technology and time-saving devices • Words with multiple definitions	• *although* • Contrasting *because* and *although* • *so* and *such*
Review: Units 5 and 6 pages 82–83		• Understanding a radio interview		
Unit 7 **Shopping** pages 84–95 Topic: **Buying and returning merchandise**	• Explaining problems with a purchase • Discussing preferences • Explaining mistakes • Asking for information about store policies	• Asking about returning merchandise • Asking about store policies • Talking about shopping mistakes • Describing people, places, and things	• Buying and returning merchandise • Compound nouns	• *that* and *who* as the subject of an adjective clause • *that* as the object of an adjective clause • Clarifying questions
Unit 8 **Work** pages 96–107 Topic: **Success at work**	• Giving advice • Making suggestions • Explaining job responsibilities • Describing the duration of an activity	• Discussing work schedules • Talking about workplace problems and their solutions • Asking questions about work experiences	• Job responsibilities and skills • Prefixes and roots	• Contrasting present perfect and present perfect continuous • Adjectives ending in *-ed* and *-ing* • Polite requests and offers
Review: Units 7 and 8 pages 108–109		• Understanding a class lecture		
Unit 9 **Daily living** pages 110–121 Topic: **Living green**	• Describing environmental issues and concerns • Giving advice • Making suggestions • Describing actions one can take	• Asking questions about "living green" • Discussing causes and effects of environmental problems • Discussing actions that could help the environment	• The environment • Antonyms	• Present unreal conditional • *since* and *so* • Contrasting present real and present unreal conditionals
Unit 10 **Free time** pages 122–133 Topic: **Celebrations**	• Describing future possibility • Describing actions based on expectations • Expressing hopes and wishes • Comparing customs and celebrations	• Asking about and comparing wedding customs • Discussing possible and hypothetical holiday plans • Talking about hopes and wishes	• Celebrations • Words with multiple meanings	• Contrasting future real and present unreal conditionals • *hope* and *wish* • Tag questions
Review: Units 9 and 10 pages 134–135		• Understanding a street interview		

READING	WRITING	LIFE SKILLS	PRONUNCIATION
■ Reading a magazine article about the impact of technology ■ Recognizing the difference between facts and opinions	■ Writing an expository paragraph about a time-saving device or activity ■ Using advantages and disadvantages to organize a paragraph	■ Using a dictionary ■ Reading and understanding a table ■ Discussing Internet use ■ Discussing survey results	■ Pronouncing key vocabulary
			■ Stressed and unstressed words
■ Reading a newspaper advice column about return policies ■ Recognizing synonyms in a reading	■ Writing a persuasive paragraph about shopping online ■ Using transition words such as *first*, *second*, *next*, *furthermore*, *moreover*, and *finally* to signal a list of reasons in a paragraph	■ Reading and understanding a returned-merchandise form ■ Talking about returning or exchanging merchandise	■ Pronouncing key vocabulary
■ Reading an article about hard and soft job skills ■ Reading a cover letter to apply for a job ■ Recognizing quotations and reasons for using them	■ Writing a cover letter to apply for a job ■ Including information about skills and experience in a cover letter	■ Using a dictionary ■ Reading and understanding a table about the fastest-growing occupations ■ Discussing work skills	■ Pronouncing key vocabulary
			■ Stressing function words
■ Reading a fable about how all things in life are connected ■ Asking questions to identify a cause-and-effect relationship	■ Writing a paragraph about an environmental problem ■ Using cause and effect to organize a paragraph	■ Using a dictionary or thesaurus ■ Reading and understanding a chart about reasons to "live green" ■ Discussing ways to help the environment	■ Pronouncing key vocabulary
■ Reading an article about special birthday celebrations around the world ■ Using punctuation as a clue to meaning	■ Writing a descriptive paragraph about a favorite holiday or celebration ■ Concluding a paragraph by relating it to your personal life	■ Using a dictionary ■ Reading and understanding a recipe ■ Discussing traditional meals and recipes	■ Pronouncing key vocabulary
			■ Linking consonant-vowel sounds

To the teacher

What is *Ventures*?

Ventures is a six-level, four-skills, standards-based, integrated-skills series that empowers students to achieve their academic and career goals.

- This most complete program with a wealth of resources provides instructors with the tools for any teaching situation.
- The new Online Workbook keeps students learning outside the classroom.
- Easy-to-teach materials make for a more productive classroom.

What components does *Ventures* have?

Student's Book with Audio CD

Each of the core **Student's Books** contains ten topic-focused units, interspersed with five review units. The main units feature six skill-focused lessons.

- **Lessons** in the Student's Book are self-contained, allowing for completion within a one-hour class period.
- **Review lessons** recycle and reinforce the listening, vocabulary, and grammar skills developed in the two prior units and include a pronunciation activity.
- **Self-assessments** in the back of the book give students an opportunity to reflect on their learning. They support learner persistence and help determine whether students are ready for the unit test.
- **Reference charts**, also in the back of the book, provide grammar paradigms and rules for spelling, punctuation, and grammar.
- References to the **Self-study audio CD** that accompanies the Student's Book are indicated in the Student's Book by an icon and track number: Look for the audio icon and track number to find activities with self-study audio. "STUDENT" refers to the self-study audio, and "CLASS" refers to the class audio. A full class audio is available separately.

  STUDENT TK 10
  CLASS CD1 TK 14

- A **Student Arcade**, available online at www.cambridge.org/venturesarcade, allows students to practice their skills with interactive activities and download self-study audio.

Teacher's Edition with Assessment Audio CD / CD-ROM

The interleaved **Teacher's Edition** includes easy-to-follow lesson plans for every unit.

- Tips and suggestions address common areas of difficulty for students and provide suggestions for expansion activities and improving learner persistence.
- A **More Ventures** chart at the end of each lesson indicates where to find additional practice material in other *Ventures* components such as the Workbook, Online Teacher's Resource Room (see below), and Student Arcade.
- Unit, midterm, and final tests, which include listening, vocabulary, grammar, reading, and writing sections, are found in the back of the Teacher's Edition.
- The **Assessment Audio CD / CD-ROM** that accompanies the Teacher's Edition contains the audio for each unit, midterm, and final test. It also features all the tests in customizable format so teachers can customize them to suit their needs.

Online Teacher's Resource Room (www.cambridge.org/myresourceroom)

Ventures 2nd Edition offers a free Online Teacher's Resource Room where teachers can download hundreds of additional worksheets and classroom materials including:

- A *placement test* that helps place students into appropriate levels of *Ventures*.
- A *Career and Educational Pathways* solution that helps students identify their educational and career goals.
- *Collaborative activities* for each lesson in Levels 1–4 that develop cooperative learning and community building within the classroom.
- *Writing worksheets* that help Literacy-level students recognize and write shapes, letters, and numbers, while alphabet and number cards promote partner and group work.
- *Picture dictionary cards and worksheets* that reinforce vocabulary learned in Levels Basic, 1, and 2.
- *Extended readings and worksheets* that provide added reading skills development for Levels 3 and 4.
- **Add Ventures** *worksheets* that were designed for use in multilevel classrooms and in leveled classes where the proficiency level of students differs.

Log on to www.cambridge.org/myresourceroom to explore these and hundreds of other free resources.

Workbook with Audio CD

The **Workbook** provides two pages of activities for each lesson in the Student's Book and includes an audio CD.

- If used in class, the Workbook can extend classroom instructional time by 30 minutes per lesson.
- The exercises are designed so learners can complete them in class or independently. Students can check their answers with the answer key in the back of the Workbook. Workbook exercises can be assigned in class, for homework, or as student support when a class is missed.
- Grammar charts at the back of the Workbook allow students to use the Workbook for self-study.

Online Workbooks

The self-grading Online Workbooks offer programs the flexibility of introducing blended learning.

- They provide the same high-quality practice opportunities as the print Workbooks and give students instant feedback.
- They allow teachers and programs to track student progress and time on task.

Unit organization

Each unit has six skill-focused lessons:

LESSON A Listening focuses students on the unit topic. The initial exercise, *Before you listen*, creates student interest with visuals that help the teacher assess what learners already know and serve as a prompt for the unit's key vocabulary. Next is *Listen*, which is based on conversations. Students relate vocabulary to meaning and relate the spoken and written forms of new theme-related vocabulary. *After you listen* concludes the lesson by practicing language related to the theme in a communicative activity, either orally with a partner or individually in a writing activity.

LESSONS B AND C focus on grammar. The lessons move from a *Grammar focus* that presents the grammar point in chart form; to *Practice* exercises that check comprehension of the grammar point and provide guided practice; and, finally, to *Communicate*

exercises that guide learners as they generate original answers and conversations. These lessons often include a *Culture note*, which provides information directly related to the conversation practice (such as the use of titles with last names), or a *Useful language* note, which introduces useful expressions and functional language.

LESSON D Reading develops reading skills and expands vocabulary. The lesson opens with a *Before you read* exercise, designed to activate prior knowledge and encourage learners to make predictions. A *Reading tip*, which focuses on a specific reading skill, accompanies the *Read* exercise. The reading section of the lesson concludes with *After you read* exercises that check comprehension. In Levels Basic, 1, and 2, the vocabulary expansion portion of the lesson is a *Picture dictionary*. It includes a *word bank*, pictures to identify, and a conversation for practicing the new words. The words expand vocabulary related to the unit topic. In Books 3 and 4, the vocabulary expansion portion of the lesson uses new vocabulary from the reading to build skills such as recognizing word families, selecting definitions based on the context of the reading, and using clues in the reading to guess meaning.

LESSON E Writing provides practice with process writing within the context of the unit. *Before you write* exercises provide warm-up activities to activate the language needed for the writing assignment, followed by one or more exercises that provide a model for students to follow when they write. A *Writing tip* presents information about punctuation or paragraph organization directly related to the writing assignment. The *Write* exercise sets goals for the student writing. In the *After you write* exercise, students share with a partner.

LESSON F Another view has three sections. *Life-skills reading* develops the scanning and skimming skills used with documents such as forms, charts, schedules, announcements, and ads. Multiple-choice questions (modeled on CASAS[1] and BEST[2]) develop test-taking skills. *Grammar connections*, in Levels 1–4, contrasts grammar points and includes guided practice and communicative activities. Finally, *Wrap up* refers students to the self-assessment page in the back of the book, where they can check their knowledge and evaluate their progress.

---

[1] The Comprehensive Adult Student Assessment System. For more information, see www.casas.org.

[2] The Basic English Skills Test. For more information, see www.cal.org/BEST.

Unit tour

The Most Complete Course for Student Success

Ventures empowers students to achieve their academic and career goals.

- The most complete program with a wealth of resources provides instructors with the tools for any teaching situation.
- The new Online Workbook keeps students learning outside the classroom.
- Easy-to-teach materials make for a more productive classroom.

The Big Picture

- Introduces the unit topic and provides rich opportunities for classroom discussion.
- Activates students' prior knowledge and previews the unit vocabulary.

Unit Goals

- Explicit unit goals ensure student involvement in the learning process.

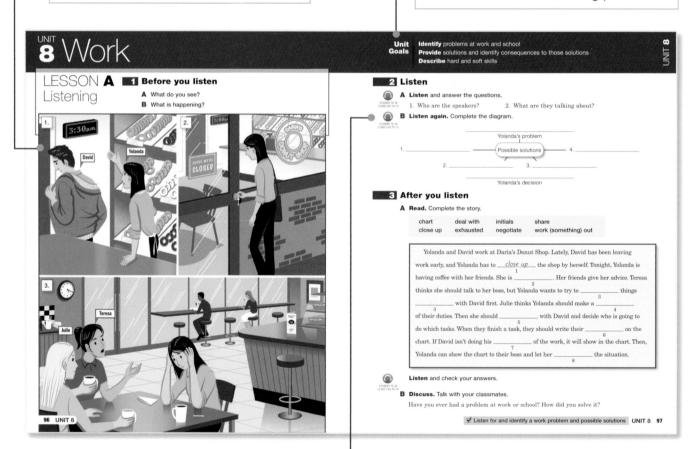

Two Different Audio Programs

- Class audio features over two hours of listening practice and improves listening comprehension.
- Self-study audio encourages learner persistence and autonomy.
- Easy navigation between the two with clear track listings.

Grammar Chart

- Clear grammar charts with additional grammar reference in the back of the book allow for greater teacher flexibility.

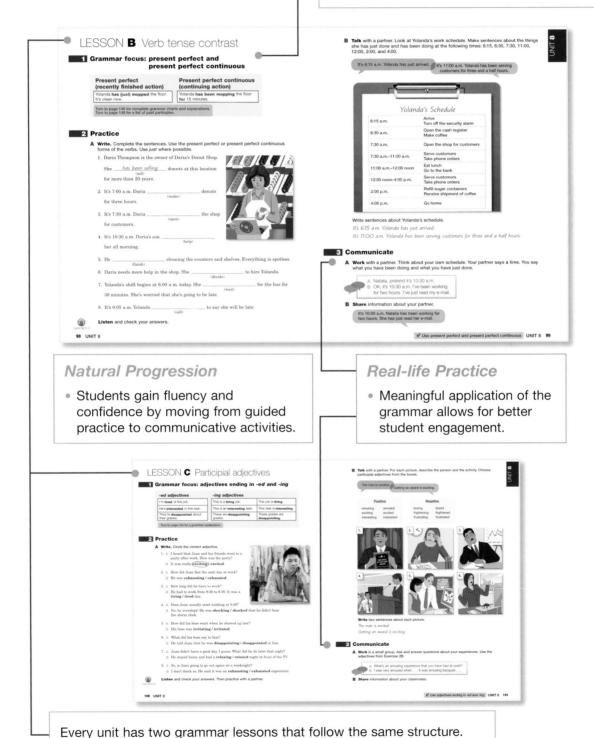

LESSON B Verb tense contrast

1 Grammar focus: present perfect and present perfect continuous

Present perfect (recently finished action)	Present perfect continuous (continuing action)
Yolanda **has (just) mopped** the floor. It's clean now.	Yolanda **has been mopping** the floor **for** 15 minutes.

Turn to page 146 for complete grammar charts and explanations.
Turn to page 149 for a list of past participles.

2 Practice

A Write. Complete the sentences. Use the present perfect or present perfect continuous forms of the verbs. Use *just* where possible.

1. Daria Thompson is the owner of Daria's Donut Shop.
She ___has been selling___ donuts at this location (sell) for more than 20 years.

2. It's 7:00 a.m. Daria _____ donuts (make) for three hours.

3. It's 7:30 a.m. Daria _____ the shop (open) for customers.

4. It's 10:30 a.m. Daria's son _____ (help) her all morning.

5. He _____ cleaning the counters and shelves. Everything is spotless. (finish)

6. Daria needs more help in the shop. She _____ to hire Yolanda. (decide)

7. Yolanda's shift begins at 6:00 a.m. today. She _____ for the bus for (wait) 30 minutes. She's worried that she's going to be late.

8. It's 6:05 a.m. Yolanda _____ to say she will be late. (call)

Listen and check your answers.

98 UNIT 8

B Talk with a partner. Look at Yolanda's work schedule. Make sentences about the things she has just done and has been doing at the following times: 6:15, 6:30, 7:30, 11:00, 12:00, 2:00, and 4:00.

> It's 6:15 a.m. Yolanda has just arrived.
> It's 11:00 a.m. Yolanda has been serving customers for three and a half hours.

Yolanda's Schedule

6:15 a.m.	Arrive / Turn off the security alarm
6:30 a.m.	Open the cash register / Make coffee
7:30 a.m.	Open the shop for customers
7:30 a.m.–11:00 a.m.	Serve customers / Take phone orders
11:00 a.m.–12:00 noon	Eat lunch / Go to the bank
12:00 noon–4:00 p.m.	Serve customers / Take phone orders
2:00 p.m.	Refill sugar containers / Receive shipment of coffee
4:00 p.m.	Go home

Write sentences about Yolanda's schedule.
It's 6:15 a.m. Yolanda has just arrived.
It's 11:00 a.m. Yolanda has been serving customers for three and a half hours.

3 Communicate

A Work with a partner. Think about your own schedule. Your partner says a time. You say what you have been doing and what you have just done.

> A Natalia, pretend it's 10:30 a.m.
> B OK, it's 10:30 a.m. I've been working for two hours. I've just read my e-mail.

B Share information about your partner.

> It's 10:30 a.m. Natalia has been working for two hours. She has just read her e-mail.

✔ Use present perfect and present perfect continuous   UNIT 8   99

Natural Progression

- Students gain fluency and confidence by moving from guided practice to communicative activities.

Real-life Practice

- Meaningful application of the grammar allows for better student engagement.

LESSON C Participial adjectives

1 Grammar focus: adjectives ending in -ed and -ing

-ed adjectives	-ing adjectives	
I'm **tired** of this job.	This is a **tiring** job.	This job is **tiring**.
He's **interested** in this task.	This is an **interesting** task.	This task is **interesting**.
They're **disappointed** about their grades.	These grades are **disappointing**.	These grades are **disappointing**.

Turn to page 146 for a grammar explanation.

2 Practice

A Write. Circle the correct adjective.

1. A I heard that Juan and his friends went to a party after work. How was the party?
   B It was really **exciting** / excited.

2. A How did Juan feel the next day at work?
   B He was **exhausting** / **exhausted**.

3. A How long did he have to work?
   B He had to work from 9:30 to 6:30. It was a **tiring** / **tired** day.

4. A Does Juan usually start working at 9:30?
   B No, he overslept! He was **shocking** / **shocked** that he didn't hear the alarm clock.

5. A How did his boss react when he showed up late?
   B His boss was **irritating** / **irritated**.

6. A What did his boss say to him?
   B He told Juan that he was **disappointing** / **disappointed** in him.

7. A Juan didn't have a good day, I guess. What did he do later that night?
   B He stayed home and had a **relaxing** / **relaxed** night in front of the TV.

8. A So, is Juan going to go out again on a weeknight?
   B I don't think so. He said it was an **exhausting** / **exhausted** experience.

Listen and check your answers. Then practice with a partner.

100 UNIT 8

B Talk with a partner. For each picture, describe the person and the activity. Choose participial adjectives from the boxes.

> The man is excited.
> Getting an award is exciting.

Positive		Negative	
amusing	amused	boring	bored
exciting	excited	frightening	frightened
interesting	interested	frustrating	frustrated

Write two sentences about each picture.
The man is excited.
Getting an award is exciting.

3 Communicate

A Work in a small group. Ask and answer questions about your experiences. Use the adjectives from Exercise 2B.

> A What's an amusing experience that you have had at work?
> B I was very amused when . . . It was amusing because . . .

B Share information about your classmates.

✔ Use adjectives ending in -ed and -ing   UNIT 8   101

Every unit has two grammar lessons that follow the same structure.

Reading

- *Ventures* features a three-step reading approach that highlights reading strategies and skills needed for success: **Before you read, Read, After you read**.

Building Vocabulary

- Explicit dictionary skills instruction expands students' vocabulary.

Integrated-skills Approach

- Reading is combined with writing and listening for an integrated approach that ensures better comprehension.

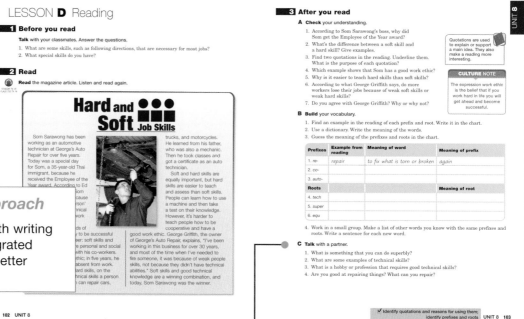

Process Writing

- *Ventures* includes a robust process-writing approach: prewriting, writing, and peer review.

Talk with a Partner

- Spoken practice helps students internalize the vocabulary and relate it to their lives.

Writing for Success

- *Ventures* writing lessons are academic and purposeful, which moves students toward work and educational goals.

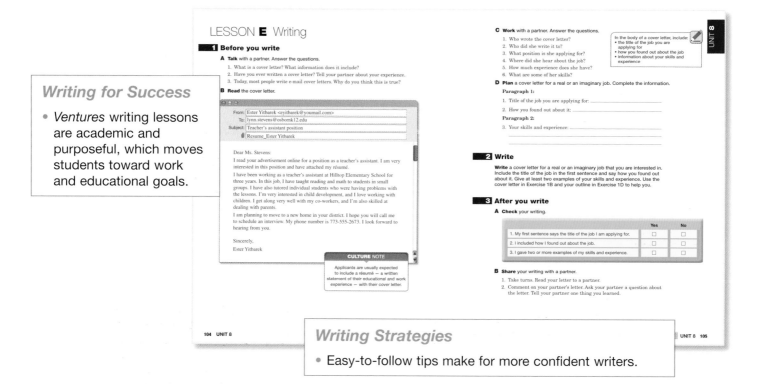

Writing Strategies

- Easy-to-follow tips make for more confident writers.

Document Literacy

- Explicit practice with authentic-type documents builds real-life skills.

Grammar Connections

- Contrasting two grammar forms in a communicative way helps with grammar accuracy.

Test-taking Skills

- Bubble answers prepare students for standardized tests like the CASAS.

Self-assessment

- Students log the vocabulary, skills, and functions they have learned for greater learner autonomy.

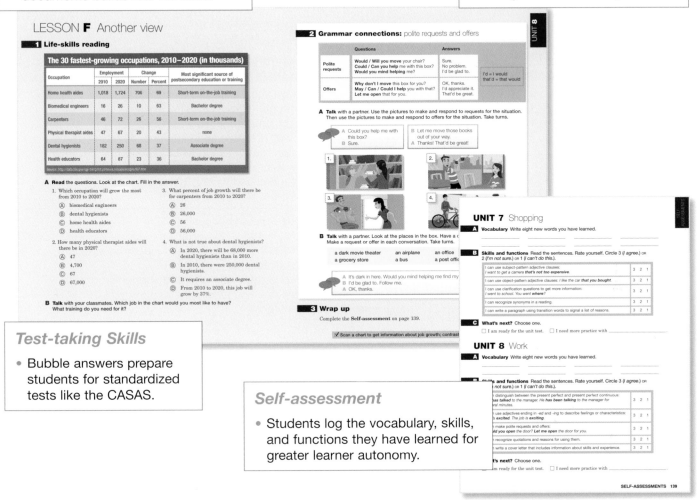

Review

- An integrated-skills approach reinforces the language of the previous two units.

Pronunciation

- An integrated-pronunciation approach promotes spoken fluency.

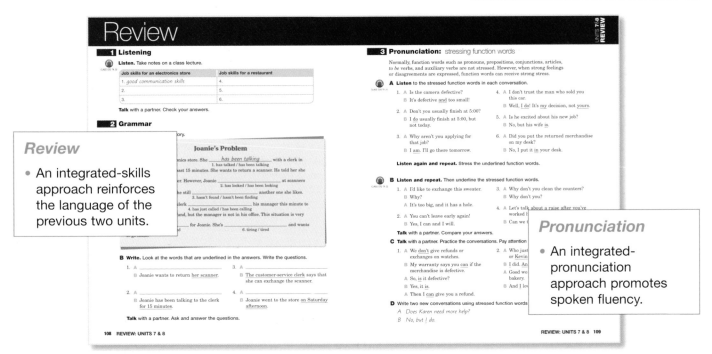

Correlations

Unit	CASAS Competencies	NRS Educational Functioning Level Descriptors *Oral BEST: 51–57 (SPL 5)* *BEST Plus: 473–506 (SPL 5)* *BEST Literacy: 54–65 (SPL 5–6)*
Unit 1 **Personal information** Pages 6–17	0.1.2, 0.1.4, 0.1.5, 0.1.6, 0.2.1, 0.2.4, 4.1.7, 4.1.8, 4.4.2, 4.5.2, 4.5.5, 4.6.1, 4.7.3, 4.8.1, 4.8.2, 7.1.1, 7.1.4, 7.2.3, 7.2.4, 7.4.1, 7.4.2, 7.4.5, 7.4.9, 7.5.1	▪ Common phrases and sentences ▪ Expanding understanding of complex grammar ▪ Reading texts on familiar subjects ▪ Reading texts with a simple and clear underlying structure ▪ Writing paragraphs with main idea and supporting details ▪ Self- and peer-edit for spelling and punctuation errors ▪ Following simple oral and written instruction
Unit 2 **At school** Pages 18–29	0.1.2, 0.1.5, 0.1.6, 0.2.1, 0.2.4, 2.3.1, 2.3.2, 2.5.5, 2.7.6, 4.1.4, 4.1.7, 4.1.9, 4.4.1, 4.6.1, 4.8.1, 4.8.2, 4.9.1, 6.0.1, 7.1.1, 7.1.4, 7.2.1, 7.2.2, 7.4.1, 7.4.2, 7.4.5, 7.5.1	▪ Common phrases and sentences ▪ Engaging in routine social conversations ▪ Reading texts with a simple and clear underlying structure ▪ Reading written directions ▪ Writing paragraphs with main idea and supporting details ▪ Following simple oral and written instruction ▪ Basic computer literacy
Unit 3 **Friends and family** Pages 32–43	0.1.2, 0.1.3, 0.1.4, 0.1.5, 0.2.2, 0.2.4, 4.4.3, 4.8.1, 4.8.2, 6.0.1, 6.6.5, 7.1.1, 7.1.4, 7.2.1, 7.2.3, 7.5.1, 7.5.5, 7.5.6, 8.3.1, 8.3.2	▪ Engaging in routine social conversations ▪ Using new vocabulary with confidence ▪ Expanding understanding of complex grammar ▪ Reading texts on familiar subjects ▪ Writing paragraphs with main idea and supporting details ▪ Self- and peer-edit for spelling and punctuation errors ▪ Following simple oral and written instruction
Unit 4 **Health** Pages 44–55	0.1.2, 0.1.3, 0.1.4, 0.1.5, 0.2.2, 0.2.4, 4.4.3, 4.8.1, 4.8.2, 6.0.1, 6.6.5, 7.1.1, 7.1.4, 7.2.1, 7.2.3, 7.5.1, 7.5.4, 7.5.5, 7.5.6, 8.3.1, 8.3.2	▪ Engaging in routine social conversations ▪ Using new vocabulary with confidence ▪ Expanding understanding of complex grammar ▪ Reading texts on familiar subjects ▪ Reading texts with a simple and clear underlying structure ▪ Writing paragraphs with main idea and supporting details ▪ Following simple oral and written instruction
Unit 5 **Around town** Pages 58–69	0.1.2, 0.1.5, 0.1.6, 0.2.4, 2.7.3, 3.1.3, 3.5.8, 3.5.9, 4.1.4, 4.8.1, 6.0.1, 7.1.1, 7.1.3, 7.1.4, 7.2.1, 7.2.2, 7.4.1, 7.4.2, 7.4.3, 7.5.1, 7.5.2, 7.5.5, 8.3.1, 8.3.2	▪ Engaging in routine social conversations ▪ Expanding understanding of complex grammar ▪ Using context to determine meaning ▪ Writing paragraphs with main idea and supporting details ▪ Self- and peer-edit for spelling and punctuation errors ▪ Following oral and written instruction ▪ Basic computer literacy

All units of *Ventures 2nd Edition* meet most of the EFF content standards and provide overall BEST test preparation. The chart above lists areas of particular focus.

For more details and correlations to other state standards, go to: www.cambridge.org/myresourceroom

EFF	Florida Adult ESOL High Intermediate	LAUSD ESL Competencies Intermediate High
▪ Conveying ideas in writing ▪ Cooperating with others ▪ Listening actively ▪ Reading with understanding ▪ Speaking so others can understand ▪ Taking responsibility for learning	5.01.01, 5.01.02, 5.01.03, 5.01.04, 5.03.06, 5.03.10, 5.03.11	A Course: I. 1b II. 5a VIII. 45 B Course: I. 1a, 1b, 1c II. 6a, 6b VIII. 35, 37, 38
▪ Attending to oral information ▪ Paying attention to the conventions of spoken English ▪ Reflecting and evaluating ▪ Selecting appropriate reading strategies ▪ Speaking so others can understand ▪ Understanding and working with pictures ▪ Cooperating with others	5.01.01, 5.01.13, 5.03.05, 5.03.06, 5.03.11, 5.03.12	A Course: II. 5a, 5b III. 11a, 11b, 11c, 15 VIII. 42, 43 B Course: II. 5, 9a III. 10a, 10b, 10c VII. 29 VIII. 35, 37, 38, 39
▪ Conveying ideas in writing ▪ Listening actively ▪ Paying attention to the conventions of spoken English ▪ Reading with understanding ▪ Resolving conflict and negotiating ▪ Taking responsibility for learning ▪ Cooperating with others ▪ Speaking so others can understand	5.01.01, 5.01.03, 5.02.08, 5.03.06, 5.03.11, 5.05.01	A Course: I. 1b II. 5a, 6 B Course: I. 2 II. 5, 6a, 7 III. 11 VIII. 37, 38
▪ Advocating and influencing ▪ Attending to oral information ▪ Cooperating with others ▪ Reading with understanding ▪ Solving problems and making decisions ▪ Speaking so others can understand	5.01.01, 5.01.03, 5.03.06, 5.03.11, 5.05.01	A Course: I. 1b B Course: II. 6c VI. 27 VIII. 37
▪ Listening actively ▪ Monitoring progress toward goals ▪ Reading with understanding ▪ Seeking feedback and revising accordingly ▪ Speaking so others can understand ▪ Understanding and working with pictures ▪ Cooperating with others	5.01.01, 5.02.07, 5.03.02, 5.03.06, 5.03.11	A Course: I. 1b VIII. 44 B Course: II. 6c III. 12, 13 VIII. 37, 40

Unit	CASAS Competencies	NRS Educational Functioning Level Descriptors *Oral BEST: 51–57 (SPL 5)* *BEST Plus: 473–506 (SPL 5)* *BEST Literacy: 54–65 (SPL 5–6)*
Unit 6 **Time** Pages 70–81	0.1.2, 0.1.5, 0.1.6, 0.2.4, 1.1.3, 1.3.1, 1.4.1, 1.7.4, 2.1.1, 2.2.3, 4.5.1, 4.5.2, 4.5.5, 4.8.1, 6.0.1, 7.1.1, 7.1.4, 7.2.1, 7.2.3, 7.2.4, 7.2.5, 7.4.1, 7.4.2, 7.4.8, 7.5.1, 7.7.1	▪ Common phrases and sentences ▪ Engaging in routine social conversations ▪ Reading texts with a simple and clear underlying structure ▪ Writing paragraphs with main idea and supporting details ▪ Following written instruction ▪ Communicating over the phone ▪ Basic computer literacy
Unit 7 **Shopping** Pages 84–95	0.1.2, 0.1.3, 0.1.5, 0.1.6, 1.2.2, 1.3.1, 1.3.3, 1.4.1, 1.6.3, 1.7.1, 4.8.1, 6.0.1, 7.1.1, 7.1.4, 7.2.1, 7.2.3, 7.2.5, 7.4.2, 7.4.3, 7.4.8, 7.5.1	▪ Using new vocabulary with confidence ▪ Expanding understanding of complex grammar ▪ Reading written directions ▪ Writing paragraphs with main idea and supporting details ▪ Self- and peer-edit for spelling and punctuation errors ▪ Following oral and written instruction ▪ Basic computer literacy
Unit 8 **Work** Pages 96–107	0.1.2, 0.1.3, 0.1.5, 0.1.7, 0.2.4, 2.3.1, 2.3.2, 2.4.1, 4.1.2, 4.1.6, 4.1.7, 4.1.8, 4.4.1, 4.4.2, 4.4.3, 4.4.4, 4.5.2, 4.5.5, 4.6.2, 4.7.3, 4.8.1, 4.8.2, 6.0.1, 7.1.1, 7.1.4, 7.2.1, 7.2.3, 7.2.7, 7.3.1, 7.3.2, 7.4.1, 7.4.2, 7.4.5, 7.5.1, 7.5.2, 7.5.6	▪ Engaging in routine social conversations ▪ Using new vocabulary with confidence ▪ Reading texts on familiar subjects ▪ Reading texts with a simple and clear underlying structure ▪ Completing job applications ▪ Practicing job-related writing ▪ Practicing job-related speaking
Unit 9 **Daily living** Pages 110–121	0.1.2, 0.1.5, 1.4.1, 2.2.3, 2.3.3, 2.7.3, 4.8.1, 5.6.1, 5.7.1, 7.1.1, 7.2.1, 7.2.2, 7.2.6, 7.3.1, 7.3.2, 7.3.4, 7.4.2, 7.4.3, 7.5.1, 7.5.4, 8.3.1	▪ Common phrases and sentences ▪ Engaging in routine social conversations ▪ Expanding understanding of complex grammar ▪ Reading texts with a simple and clear underlying structure ▪ Reading written directions ▪ Writing paragraphs with main idea and supporting details ▪ Following simple oral and written instruction
Unit 10 **Free time** Pages 122–133	0.1.1, 0.1.2, 0.1.5, 0.1.6, 0.2.4, 1.1.1, 1.1.5, 2.3.2, 2.5.7, 2.7.1, 2.7.2, 2.7.4, 4.5.2, 4.5.5, 4.8.1, 6.0.1, 7.1.1, 7.1.4, 7.2.1, 7.2.3, 7.2.4, 7.2.6, 7.4.1, 7.4.2, 7.4.4, 7.4.5, 7.5.1, 7.5.6	▪ Engaging in routine social conversations ▪ Using new vocabulary with confidence ▪ Expanding understanding of complex grammar ▪ Reading texts on familiar subjects ▪ Reading written directions ▪ Writing paragraphs with main idea and supporting details ▪ Following simple oral and written instruction

All units of *Ventures 2nd Edition* meet most of the EFF content standards and provide overall BEST test preparation. The chart above lists areas of particular focus.

For more details and correlations to other state standards, go to: www.cambridge.org/myresourceroom

EFF	Florida Adult ESOL High Intermediate	LAUSD ESL Competencies Intermediate High
■ Conveying ideas in writing ■ Cooperating with others ■ Listening actively ■ Reading with understanding ■ Speaking so others can understand ■ Using information and communications technology	5.01.01, 5.01.02, 5.01.03, 5.03.02, 5.03.06, 5.03.11, 5.03.15	A Course: II. 5a B Course: II. 6a, 6b VIII. 37, 38
■ Advocating and influencing ■ Attending to oral information ■ Reflecting and evaluating ■ Selecting appropriate reading strategies ■ Solving problems and making decisions ■ Taking responsibility for learning ■ Cooperating with others ■ Speaking so others can understand	5.01.01, 5.03.02, 5.03.06, 5.03.11, 5.04.02, 5.04.09	A Course: IV. 21a B Course: VIII. 37
■ Attending to oral information ■ Monitoring comprehension and adjusting reading strategies ■ Paying attention to the conventions of spoken English ■ Seeking input from others ■ Taking stock of where one is ■ Understanding and working with pictures ■ Cooperating with others ■ Speaking so others can understand	5.01.01, 5.01.03, 5.03.02, 5.03.03, 5.03.06, 5.03.07, 5.03.11, 5.03.13	A Course: I. 4b VII. 34, 38a, 38b, 38c, 41 B Course: VIII. 37, 38, 41
■ Conveying ideas in writing ■ Guiding others ■ Listening actively ■ Reading with understanding ■ Solving problems and making decisions ■ Speaking so others can understand ■ Cooperating with others	5.01.01, 5.01.03, 5.02.02, 5.03.06, 5.03.11	B Course: II. 7 VIII. 37, 38
■ Attending to oral information ■ Attending to visual sources of information ■ Interacting with others in positive ways ■ Paying attention to the conventions of written English ■ Reading with understanding ■ Selecting appropriate reading strategies ■ Cooperating with others ■ Speaking so others can understand	5.01.01, 5.01.03, 5.02.03, 5.03.06, 5.03.11	A Course: II. 5b B Course: II. 6b, 7, 9 VIII. 37, 38, 40

Meet the *Ventures* author team

Gretchen Bitterlin has been an ESL teacher and an ESL department chair. She is currently the ESL coordinator for the Continuing Education Program at San Diego Community College District. Under Gretchen's leadership, the ESL program has developed several products – for example, an ESL oral interview placement test and writing rubrics for assessing writing for level exit – now used by other agencies. She is a co-author of *English for Adult Competency*, has been an item writer for CASAS tests, and chaired the task force that developed the TESOL *Adult Education Program Standards*. She is a recipient of her district's award, Outstanding Contract Faculty. Gretchen holds an MA in TESOL from the University of Arizona.

Dennis Johnson had his first language-teaching experience as a Peace Corps volunteer in South Korea. Following that teaching experience, he became an in-country ESL trainer. After returning to the United States, he became an ESL trainer and began teaching credit and non-credit ESL at City College of San Francisco. As ESL site coordinator, he has provided guidance to faculty in selecting textbooks. He is the author of *Get Up and Go* and co-author of *The Immigrant Experience*. Dennis is the demonstration teacher on the *Ventures Professional Development DVD*. Dennis holds an MA in music from Stanford University.

Donna Price began her ESL career teaching EFL in Madagascar. She is currently associate professor of ESL and vocational ESL / technology resource instructor for the Continuing Education Program, San Diego Community College District. She has served as an author and a trainer for CALPRO, the California Adult Literacy Professional Development Project, co-authoring training modules on contextualizing and integrating workforce skills into the ESL classroom. She is a recipient of the TESOL Newbury House Award for Excellence in Teaching, and she is author of *Skills for Success*. Donna holds an MA in linguistics from San Diego State University.

Sylvia Ramirez started as an instructional aide in ESL. Since then she has been a part-time teacher, a full-time teacher, and a program coordinator. As program coordinator at Mira Costa College, she provided leadership in establishing Managed Enrollment, Student Learning Outcomes, and Transitioning Adults to Academic and Career Preparation. Her more than forty years in adult ESL includes multilevel ESL, vocational ESL, family literacy, and distance learning. She has also provided technical assistance to local ESL programs for the California State Department of Education. In 2011 she received the Hayward Award in education. Her MA is in education / counseling from Point Loma University, and she has certificates in TESOL and in online teaching.

K. Lynn Savage first taught English in Japan. She began teaching ESL at City College of San Francisco in 1974, where she has taught all levels of non-credit ESL and has served as vocational ESL resource teacher. She has trained teachers for adult education programs around the country as well as abroad. She chaired the committee that developed *ESL Model Standards for Adult Education Programs* (California, 1992) and is the author, co-author, and editor of many ESL materials including *Crossroads Café, Teacher Training through Video, Parenting for Academic Success, Building Life Skills, Picture Stories, May I Help You?*, and *English That Works*. Lynn holds an MA in TESOL from Teachers College, Columbia University.

To the student

Welcome to **Ventures**! The dictionary says that "venture" means a risky or daring journey. Its meaning is similar to the word "adventure." Learning English is certainly a journey and an adventure. We hope that this book helps you in your journey of learning English to fulfill your goals. We believe that this book will prepare you for academic and career courses and give you the English skills you need to get a job or promotion, go to college, or communicate better in your community. The CDs, the Workbooks, and the free Internet practice on the Arcade will help you improve your English outside class. Setting your personal goals will also help. Take a few minutes and write down your goals below.

Good luck in your studies!

The Author Team
Gretchen Bitterlin
Dennis Johnson
Donna Price
Sylvia Ramirez
K. Lynn Savage

My goals for studying English

1. My first goal for studying English:	Date: _____
2. My second goal for studying English:	Date: _____
3. My third goal for studying English:	Date: _____

Welcome

1 Meet your classmates

A Look at the picture. What do you see?

B What are the people doing?

2 Study habits and strategies

STUDENT TK 2
CLASS CD1 TK 2

A Listen. Check (✓) the adjectives, study habits, and strategies you hear.

☐ active	☐ creative	☐ outgoing	☐ study in a group
☐ artistic	☐ fun-loving	☐ patient	☐ study while moving
☐ confident	☑ make vocabulary cards	☐ reliable	☐ use a dictionary

Listen again. Check your answers.

B Read the list of study habits and strategies. Which ones have you tried?
Check (✓) your answers on the chart. Then tell a partner about your answers.

Have you ever . . . ?	Yes, I have.	No, I haven't.
1. made vocabulary cards		
2. used a dictionary to learn new words		
3. asked a stranger a question in English		
4. studied English with a friend		
5. used a to-do list to organize your time		
6. tried to guess the meaning of new words		

C Talk with your classmates. Complete the chart.

> A Song-mi, do you watch TV in English every day?
> B Yes, I do.

Find a classmate who . . .	Name
1. watches TV in English every day	Song-mi
2. asks questions when he or she doesn't understand something	
3. underlines important information in textbooks	
4. likes to sing songs	
5. speaks English at work	
6. sets goals for learning English	

Talk with your class. Ask and answer questions.

Who watches TV in English every day?

Song Mi does.

Manny does, too.

3 Verb tense review (past continuous and simple past)

A **Listen** to each sentence. Circle the verb form you hear.

1. listened   was listening   5. played   was playing
2. heard   was hearing   6. did   were doing
3. watched   was watching   7. drove   were driving
4. woke   were waking   8. vacuumed   were vacuuming

Listen again. Check your answers.

B **Read.** Complete the story. Use the correct verb form.

Last summer, my sister and I _____*drove*_____ from Tucson to Phoenix.
                                    1. drive

On our way, it _____ very windy, and there _____
                    2. be   3. be

dark clouds in the sky. We _____ slowly when suddenly we
                                4. travel

_____ huge clouds of dust in the air. The sky _____
      5. see   6. turn

brown, and we couldn't see anything. It _____ very scary.
                                              7. be

While we _____, we _____ for a place to turn off
              8. drive   9. look

the road. Finally we _____ to an exit and _____
                          10. come   11. get

off the main road. We _____ into a restaurant. The dust finally
                            12. go

_____ away while we _____ at the restaurant.
      13. go   14. wait

Listen and check your answers.

C **Talk** with a partner. Ask and answer questions.

1. Talk about a time you were in bad weather. Describe the weather. Explain what happened.
2. What were you doing before the bad weather started?
3. What did you do while the bad weather was happening?

4 WELCOME

4 Verb tense review (simple past and present perfect)

A Listen to each sentence. Check (✓) the correct column.

STUDENT TK 5
CLASS CD1 TK 5

	Past	Present perfect		Past	Present perfect
1.	✓		6.		
2.			7.		
3.			8.		
4.			9.		
5.			10.		

Listen and check your answers.

B Read. Complete the conversations. Use the simple past or present perfect form of the verb in parentheses.

1. A ____Have____ you ever __practiced__ English with a conversation partner? (practice)

   B No, I __haven't__. I'm too shy.

2. A _____ you _____ to the theater last night? (go)

   B Yes, I _____. The movie was great.

3. A _____ you ever _____ dancing in a night club? (go)

   B No, I _____. I'm not very outgoing.

4. A _____ Daniel _____ at the elementary school yesterday? (volunteer)

   B Yes, he _____. He is very reliable.

5. A _____ your son ever _____ in a school play? (be)

   B Yes, he _____. He's very enthusiastic about acting.

Listen and check your answers.

STUDENT TK 6
CLASS CD1 TK 6

C Talk with your classmates. Ask and answer the questions.

1. Have you ever volunteered? What did you do?
2. Do you ever go dancing? Where do you go?
3. Have you ever asked a stranger a question in English? What did you ask?

LESSON A
Listening

1 Before you listen

A What do you see?

B What is happening?

1. Emily / Nina
2. Brenda
3. Gerry
4. Danny

Unit Goals	**Identify** multiple intelligences
	Identify one's primary intelligence
	Recognize right-brain and left-brain functions

2 Listen

A Listen and answer the questions.

1. Who are the speakers?   2. What are they talking about?

STUDENT TK 7
CLASS CD1 TK 7

B Listen again. Complete the chart.

STUDENT TK 7
CLASS CD1 TK 7

Family member	Good at	Example
1. Brenda	*math*	*got first place in a math contest*
2. Gerry		
3. Danny		
4. Nina		

3 After you listen

A Read. Complete the story.

aptitude⁸   bright³   gifted in⁴   mechanical⁴

brain²   fixing up⁷   mathematical¹   musical⁵

Emily stops by Nina's house on her way home from jogging. They talk about Nina's

three children. Brenda is very _mathematical_. She's just won a math contest at school. When
                                    1

Emily calls Brenda a _____, Nina says that all her children are _____, but
                            2   3

in different ways. Gerry isn't _____ math, but he's very _____. He plays
                                    4   5

and sings very well and even writes music. Danny is the _____ one in the family.
                                                                6

He's good at _____ old cars. Emily thinks that Nina is also smart because she is
                    7

such a good cook. Emily has no _____ for cooking.
                                    8

Listen and check your answers.

STUDENT TK 8
CLASS CD1 TK 8

B Discuss. Talk with your classmates.

1. How are the three children different?
2. Do you think that one child is more intelligent than the others? Why or why not?
3. Do you think that Nina is a good parent? Why or why not?

LESSON **B** Parts of speech

1 Grammar focus: nouns, verbs, adjectives, and adverbs

Adjective + Noun
Helen is an **intelligent girl**.
I am a **slow driver**.
It was a very **easy game**.
You're a **good dancer**.

Verb + Adverb
She **talks intelligently**.
I **drive slowly**.
He **won** very **easily**.
You **dance well**.

> **USEFUL** LANGUAGE
>
> Ask *How?* to identify adverbs.
> (*How does she drive?*)
> Ask *What kind of?*
> to identify adjectives.
> (*What kind of driver is she?*)

Irregular	
Adjectives	**Adverbs**
fast	fast
good	well
hard	hard

Turn to page 141 for a grammar explanation.

2 Practice

A Write. Complete the sentences with adjectives or adverbs. Underline the nouns and verbs that they describe.

1. Carol speaks very ___intelligently___ . She's a ___bright___ girl.
   (intelligent)   (bright)

2. That isn't a _____ guitar, but he's playing it _____ .
   (bad)   (bad)

3. Benny is an _____ cook. His dinner last night was _____ .
   (excellent)   (fantastic)

4. The mechanic did a _____ job on my car. Now it runs _____ .
   (good)   (perfect)

5. You danced very _____ in the dance contest. You are a _____ dancer!
   (skillful)   (wonderful)

6. I don't type very _____ . I can't move my fingers very _____ .
   (fast)   (quick)

7. That writing test was _____ . Writing is not an _____ subject for me.
   (hard)   (easy)

8. You sang that song _____ ! I didn't know you could sing so _____ !
   (beautiful)   (good)

9. Your report is _____ . You wrote it very _____ .
   (great)   (clear)

10. I work _____ . I am a _____ worker.
    (slow)   (careful)

 Listen and check your answers.

B Talk with a partner. Ask and answer questions about the pictures. Use the adjective or adverb form of the words in the box.

A What kind of artist is he?	A How does he paint?
B He's a skillful artist.	B He paints beautifully.

beautiful	excellent	good	skillful
careful	fast	professional	wonderful

1. artist / paint

2. seamstress / sew

3. driver / drive

4. carpenter / work

5. singer / sing

6. dancers / dance

Write sentences about the people.

He's a skillful artist. He paints beautifully.

3 Communicate

A Work in a small group. Ask and answer the questions.

1. What kind of student are you?
2. How do you speak English?
3. What can you do very well?
4. What kind of worker are you?
5. What can you do perfectly?
6. What do you do very fast?

B Share information about your classmates.

> Armando says he's an excellent student.

LESSON C Noun clauses

1 Grammar focus: *that* clauses as objects

Statements and questions

Emily realizes **that Brenda has a good brain**.
People say **that Gerry plays the guitar very well**.
Do you think **that people are smart in different ways**?
Do you feel **that you're smart**?

Introductory clauses

I think . . .	Do you think . . . ?
I feel . . .	Do you feel . . . ?
He realizes . . .	Does he realize . . . ?
People believe . . .	Do people believe . . . ?

Turn to page 141 for a complete grammar chart and explanation.

Turn to page 141 for a complete grammar chart and explanation.

> **USEFUL** LANGUAGE
>
> When speaking, we frequently omit *that* before a noun clause.
> *People think **that** she's smart.*
> *People think she's smart.*

2 Practice

A **Write.** Write sentences with *that* and a noun clause. Circle the noun clause in your sentence.

1. There are many kinds of intelligence. (Do you believe . . . ?)

   Do you believe (that there are many kinds of intelligence)?

2. Nina has an interesting family. (Do you think . . . ?)

   _____

3. She is very gifted in math. (Brenda's teacher agrees . . .)

   _____

4. Gerry will be a famous musician someday. (Everyone believes . . .)

   _____

5. Danny has an aptitude for fixing up cars. (I didn't realize . . .)

   _____

6. Mechanical skills are very important. (Do you feel . . . ?)

   _____

7. Nina is a good cook. (Do you think . . . ?)

   _____

Listen and check your answers.

CLASS CD1 TK 10

B **Talk** with a partner. Look at the picture. Answer the questions. Use introductory clauses from the box.

Robert   Anna   Tomas

| I believe . . . | I suppose . . . | I think . . . | I'd say . . . | I'm sure . . . |

A I think (that) Robert is about 26 years old.
B I'd say (that) Robert is only 20.

1. How old are they?
2. Where are they going?
3. Where are they coming from?
4. What do they do for a living?
5. What are they good at?
6. What aren't they good at?

Write sentences about your opinions.

I think that Robert is about 26 years old.

3 Communicate

A **Work** in a small group. Give your opinions. Use *I believe, I think, I'd say, I don't believe,* and other introductory clauses.

1. Are women more talkative than men?
2. Are boys better at math and science than girls?
3. Are men more mechanical than women?
4. Are women more musical than men?
5. Are men more interested in sports than women?
6. Can women do the same jobs as men?

B **Share** your classmates' opinions.

Marta thinks that women are more talkative than men.

USEFUL LANGUAGE

I (totally) agree with you.
I (strongly) disagree.

CULTURE NOTE

Studies have shown that girls and boys in the United States have a similar aptitude for math and science when they start elementary school.

LESSON **D** Reading

▌1 **Before you read**

Talk with a partner. Look at the reading tip. Answer the questions.

1. What is this article about?
2. According to the article, how many ways are there to be smart?

▌2 **Read**

STUDENT TK 9
CLASS CD1 TK 11

 Read the magazine article. Listen and read again.

> Before you begin reading, **skim**. Look at the title, headings, and boldfaced words to get a general idea of what the reading is about.

Many Ways to be **SMART**

Josh is a star on the school baseball team. He gets Ds and Fs on all his math tests. His brother Frank can't catch, throw, or hit a baseball, but he easily gets As in math. Which boy do you think is more intelligent? Howard Gardner, a professor of education at Harvard University, would say that Josh and Frank are both smart, but in different ways. His theory of multiple intelligences identifies eight different "intelligences" to explain the way people understand, experience, and learn about the world around them.

 Verbal / Linguistic
Some people are good with words. They prefer to learn by reading, listening, and speaking.

 Bodily / Kinesthetic
Some people are "body smart." They are often athletic. Kinesthetic learners learn best when they are moving.

 Logical / Mathematical
These people have an aptitude for math. They like solving logic problems and puzzles.

 Interpersonal
Certain people are "group smart." They easily understand other people. They are good at communicating and interacting with others.

 Musical / Rhythmical
These people are sensitive to sound, melodies, and rhythms. They are gifted in singing, playing instruments, or composing music.

 Intrapersonal
Some people are "self smart." They can understand their own feelings and emotions. They often enjoy spending time alone.

 Visual / Spatial
These "picture people" are often good at drawing or painting. They are sensitive to colors and designs.

 Naturalist
These people are skilled in working with plants and animals in the natural world.

According to Gardner, many people have several or even all of these intelligences, but most of us have one or two intelligences that are primary, or strongest.

3 After you read

A **Check** your understanding. Which primary intelligence do these people have?

1. Josh Dillon, age 16: A star on the school baseball team; loves all sports; plans to become a coach.	*bodily / kinesthetic*
2. Ida Grove, age 45: Knows the name of everything in her garden.	Naturalist
3. Manisha Pari, age 22: Writes in her journal every day about her feelings; enjoys taking walks by herself.	intrapersonal
4. Joy Rhee, age 30: Writes short stories and enjoys poetry.	Verbal / Linguitic
5. Susana Ochoa, age 42: Vocational counselor at a community college; volunteers at her church every Sunday.	Interpersonal
6. Amal Mohammed, age 27: Photographer; takes art classes.	Visual / spatial

B **Build** your vocabulary.

Understanding prefixes and roots of words will help you learn new words.
1. Find an example of each prefix or root in the reading. Write it on the chart.
2. Use a dictionary. Write the meaning of the words.
3. Guess the meaning of the prefixes and roots on the chart.

Prefixes	Example from reading	Meaning of word	Meaning of prefix
1. *intra-*	*intrapersonal*	*inside a person's mind or self*	*in, inside*
2. *inter-*	interpersonal	between person	between
3. *multi-*	multiple	many	
Roots			**Meaning of root**
4. *kine*	motion		
5. *log*	word		
6. *prim*	first		
7. *vis*	See		

C **Talk** with a partner.

1. What is your primary intelligence?
2. What are good jobs for people with each of the following intelligences: intrapersonal, interpersonal, kinesthetic, logical, and visual?

☑ Skim an article for the main idea before reading; use prefixes and roots to find the meaning of words   **UNIT 1   13**

LESSON E Writing

1 Before you write

A **Write** *1* through *4* next to your strongest intelligences. (Your primary intelligence should be number 1.) Compare with your classmates.

_____ Verbal / Linguistic   _3_ Bodily / Kinesthetic

_____ Logical / Mathematical   _2_ Interpersonal

_4_ Musical / Rhythmical   _____ Intrapersonal

_____ Visual / Spatial   _1_ Naturalist

B **Read** the writing tip. Then read the paragraphs. Choose the best topic sentence for each paragraph. Write it on the line.

1. Topic sentence:

a. I enjoy taking my flute to the park.

b. My primary intelligence is musical.

> *Main/most important*
>
> The <u>topic</u> sentence tells what the paragraph is about. A good paragraph has a topic sentence and supporting sentences.

My primary intelligence is musical. All my life, I've enjoyed singing and playing the flute. While I was growing up, my favorite classes were always music classes. I've taken private music lessons and also attended special summer music camps. I think that I can play well, and I also like to write original songs. On weekends, I enjoy taking my flute to a nearby park. There, I sit on the grass and play for hours. If I'm not playing, I'm listening to the music of the birds and the wind in the trees.

2. Topic sentence:

a. My strongest intelligence is mathematical.

b. In school, my favorite subject was mathematics.

My strongest intelligence is mathematical. My parents say that I started counting before I was two years old. I've always liked to play games with numbers. I never forget my friends' birthdays or telephone numbers. I like to keep track of my monthly expenses so that I stay within my budget. Other people complain that balancing their checkbooks is hard, but I enjoy it. My aptitude for mathematics helps me in every part of my life.

C **Complete** the outline.

Read these supporting details about a person with kinesthetic intelligence.
Write a topic sentence.

Topic sentence: _His primary intelligence is kinesthetic ._

Supporting details:

- Since I was a child, I have loved to move my body. *kinesthetic*
- I've taken many types of dance classes, including ballet, modern, jazz, swing, salsa, and African. *Bodily/ kinesthetic*
- I can dance to any kind of music that I hear. *kinesthetic*
- My friends say that I'm a great dancer. *kinesthetic*

D **Plan** a paragraph about your primary intelligence. Use the outline to make notes on your ideas.

Topic sentence: _My primary intelligence is naturalist ._

Supporting details:

- _I enjoyed grown up flowers anywhere in the garden ._
- _I've taken many types of plants including flowers. friut trees_
- _and some vegetables ._
- _When I was a child. I like to watered for the plants ._
- _____

2 Write

Write a paragraph about your primary intelligence. Include a general topic sentence that tells what your paragraph is about. Give specific details to support it. Use the paragraphs in Exercise 1B and the outlines in Exercises 1C and 1D to help you.

3 After you write

A **Check** your writing.

	Yes	No
1. My paragraph starts with a general topic sentence.	☐	☐
2. My topic sentence tells what my paragraph is about.	☐	☐
3. I gave specific details to support my topic sentence.	☐	☐

B **Share** your writing with a partner.

1. Take turns. Read your paragraph to a partner.
2. Comment on your partner's paragraph. Ask your partner a question about the paragraph. Tell your partner one thing you learned.

LESSON F Another view

1 Life-skills reading

Left-brain functions   **Right-brain functions**

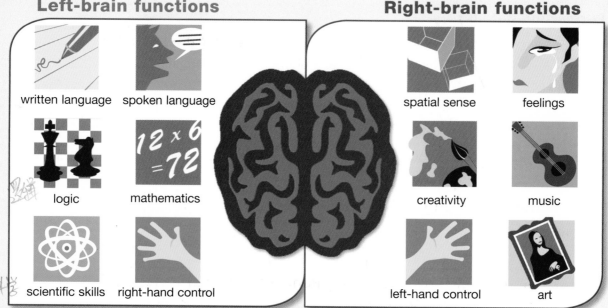

written language   spoken language   spatial sense   feelings

logic   mathematics   creativity   music

scientific skills   right-hand control   left-hand control   art

A **Read** the questions. Look at the diagram. Fill in the answer.

1. Which side of the brain controls verbal ability?
   - ● left side
   - Ⓑ right side
   - Ⓒ both sides
   - Ⓓ none of the above

2. Which abilities are right-brain functions?
   - Ⓐ art
   - Ⓑ music
   - Ⓒ creativity
   - Ⓓ all of the above

3. Which ability is not a left-brain function?
   - Ⓐ scientific skills
   - Ⓑ feelings
   - Ⓒ spoken language
   - Ⓓ none of the above

4. Which sentence is true?
   - Ⓐ The left brain controls the left hand.
   - Ⓑ The right brain controls the right hand.
   - Ⓒ The left brain controls the right hand.
   - Ⓓ none of the above

5. What can you say about "left-brained" people?
   - Ⓐ They are left-handed.
   - Ⓑ They are very musical.
   - Ⓒ They are artistic.
   - Ⓓ They are logical.

6. Which intelligence is a right-brain intelligence?
   - Ⓐ musical / rhythmical
   - Ⓑ logical / mathematical
   - Ⓒ linguistic / verbal
   - Ⓓ both a and b

B **Talk** with a partner. Are you a right-brained or a left-brained person? What about the other people in your family?

2 Grammar connections: *so* and *that*

	Yes answer	*No answer*
Do you think **that** math is essential to succeed at school? 成功、继续 lisen到||水要知、基本功	Yes, I think **so**. (I think **that** math is essential to succeed at school.)	No, I don't think **so**. (I don't think **that** math is essential to succeed at school.)
Does Maria think **that** robots will do most of the work in the future?	Yes, she hopes **so**. (She hopes **that** robots will do most of the work in the future.)	No, she hopes **not**. (She hopes **that** robots won't do most of the work in the future.)

A **Work** in a small group. Ask and answer the questions. Give reasons. Then complete the chart with your classmates' answers.

> A Do you think that there will be only one world language in the future?
> B No, I don't think so. There are too many people in small villages around the world. It would be difficult to get everyone to learn the same language.
> C Yes, I hope so . . .

Do you think that . . .	Lina (name)	(name)	(name)	(name)
1. it's easy to find a job?	No			
2. people waste too much time on the Internet?	Yes			
3. there will be only one world language in the future?	No			
4. more women will study science in the future?	Yes			
5. most people will live to be 100 in the future?	Yes			
6. cell phones will get smaller?	No			

B **Talk** with a new partner. Ask and answer questions about your classmates.

> A Does Lina think that there will be only one world language?
> B No, she doesn't think so.

3 Wrap up

Complete the **Self-assessment** on page 136.

☑ Scan a diagram for information about brain functions; use *so* and *that* in questions and answers   **UNIT 1   17**

LESSON **A**
Listening

1 **Before you listen**

A What do you see?

B What is happening?

1.

Vasili

2.

Hospitality & Tourism
Certificate Program
REGISTER NOW!
See your counselor
for more information!

Mrs. Ochoa

Unit Goals	**Make** educational plans
	Write a descriptive paragraph about a successful person
	Scan a chart for the location of classes

UNIT 2

2 Listen

STUDENT TK 10
CLASS CD1 TK 12

A Listen and answer the questions.

1. Who are the speakers?   2. What are they talking about?

STUDENT TK 10
CLASS CD1 TK 12

B Listen again. Complete the chart.

1. Type of certificate	*Hospitality and Tourism*
2. Places of employment	hotels. restaurants. airlines.
3. Number of required classes	Six of required classes
4. Time to complete the program	one or two years
5. Cost per unit	Fifty dollars.
6. Estimated cost to earn the certificate	sixteen hundred / one thousand six hundred.

3 After you listen

A Read. Complete the story.

| bilingual | high-paying | internship | qualify |
| deadline | industry | motivated | requirements |

> Vasili hears a radio ad about the Hospitality and Tourism Certificate Program at La Costa Community College. The ad says graduates can find __high-paying__ jobs
> (1)
> in the tourism __industry__. Vasili goes to see his ESL counselor, Mrs. Ochoa. She
> (2)
> tells him about the program __requirements__, which include an __intership__ in a local
> (3)   (4)
> tourism business. She also tells him about the __deadline__ for registration, and she
> (5)
> says there is financial aid for students who __qualify__. Vasili is concerned about
> (6)
> his English, but Mrs. Ochoa tells him not to worry. Vasili is __bilingual__, he's very
> (7)
> __motivated__, and he has good interpersonal skills.
> (8)

STUDENT TK 11
CLASS CD1 TK 13

Listen and check your answers.

B Discuss. Talk with your classmates. Is hospitality and tourism a good industry for Vasili? Would you like this type of career? Why or why not?

LESSON **B** The passive

1 Grammar focus: present passive

Active 主动	**Present passive** 现在被动
The college **gives** a placement test.	A placement test **is given** (by the college).
The college **offers** online classes every semester.	Online classes **are offered** (by the college) every semester.
Does the college **offer** financial aid?	**Is** financial aid **offered** (by the college)?
When **does** the college **arrange** internships?	When **are** internships **arranged** (by the college)?

Turn to page 142 for a complete grammar chart and explanation.
Turn to page 149 for a list of past participles.

Turn to page 142 for a complete grammar chart and explanation.
Turn to page 149 for a list of past participles.

2 Practice

A Write. Complete the sentences. Use the present passive.

1. **A** When _____*is*_____ the English placement test _____*given*_____ to new students?
 (give)

   B The English placement test ___*is administered*___ a week before the first day of class.
 (administer)

2. **A** ___*Is*___ a math placement test also ___*required*___ ?
 (require)

   B No, a math placement test ___*is*___ not ___*needed*___ .
 (need)

3. **A** Where ___*is*___ the financial aid office ___*located*___ ?
 (locate)

   B It ___*is located*___ next to the admissions office.
 (locate)

4. **A** Where ___*are*___ the classes ___*held*___ ?
 (hold)

   B Most of the classes ___*are held*___ in the business building.
 (hold)

5. **A** ___*Are*___ classes ___*offered*___ at different times?
 (offer)

   B Yes. Both day and evening classes ___*are offered*___ .
 (offer)

6. **A** ___*Are*___ job placement services ___*provided*___ to graduates?
 (provide)

   B Yes. Job help ___*is offered*___ to students who qualify.
 (offer)

 Listen and check your answers. Then practice with a partner.

CLASS CD1 TK 14

B **Talk** with a partner. Read about two courses in the Hospitality and Tourism Certificate Program. Ask and answer questions using the present passive. Use the past participles in the box.

| given | held | located | offered | required |

> **A** When is Hospitality 100 offered?
> **B** It's offered in the fall and spring.

> **A** Are day and evening classes given?
> **B** Yes, they are.

La Costa Community College Course Schedule
Hospitality and Tourism Certificate Program

HOSP 100: Introduction to Hospitality and Tourism

Requirement: Pass English placement test. Fall and spring
T / Th 10:00–11:30 a.m.
M / W 6:00–7:30 p.m.

Room: T130

BUS 137: Customer Service

Requirement: Pass HOSP 100. Spring
T / Th 8:00–9:30 a.m.
(Online course also available.)

Room: B480

Write sentences about the courses.

Hospitality 100 is offered in the fall and spring.

3 Communicate

A **Work** with a partner. Role-play a conversation between a counselor and a student who wants to enroll in a certificate program at your school. Ask and answer questions about the topics below. Predict the answers a counselor would give.

- online courses
- required courses
- English or math placement tests
- location of classes

- internships
- financial aid
- job counseling

> **Student** Are online courses offered in the certificate program?
> **Counselor** No. Online courses are not offered in that program.
> **Student** What about internships?
> **Counselor** Internships are arranged for each student in the program.

B **Perform** your role play for the class.

LESSON C The passive

1 Grammar focus: infinitives after the passive

	Verbs often followed by infinitives
Students **are told to arrive** early on the first day of class.	advise
Everyone **is encouraged to attend** class regularly.	encourage
Are students **required to do** homework every night?	expect
How often **are** students **expected to meet** with their counselors?	require tell

Turn to page 142 for a grammar explanation.

2 Practice

A Write complete statements or questions. Use the present passive with infinitives.

1. applicants / expect / meet / all application deadlines.

   Applicants are expected to meet all application deadlines.

2. new students / tell / come early / for registration.

   New students are told to come early for registration.

3. all new students / require / take / a writing test?

   Are all new students required to take a writing test?

4. some students / advise / enroll / in an English composition class.

   Some students are advised to enroll in an English composition class.

5. students / expect / attend / every class?

   Are students expected to attend every class?

6. students / encourage / meet / with a counselor regularly.

   Students are encouraged to meet with a counselor regularly.

7. when / participants / expect / complete / their internships?

   When are participants expected to complete their internships?

8. students / require / earn / a grade of C or better in each course.

   Students are required to earn a grade of C or better in each course.

9. students / tell / study / with a partner and to go to tutoring often.

   Students are told to study with a partner and to go to tutoring often.

Listen and check your answers.

CLASS CD1 TK 15

B **Talk** with a partner. Read the ad. Make statements about the Work Experience Program at La Costa Community College. Use the past participles in the box.

> Students are allowed to earn college credit for work experience.

advised	asked	expected	reminded	told
allowed	encouraged	permitted	required	

Work Experience Program at La Costa Community College

Earn college credit for the job you have.

You can earn up to 4 units of credit by participating in the program.

To enroll, attend an orientation session. Then work at least 75 paid hours or 60 volunteer hours. Questions?

Contact the Career Center at 777-555-2222, or visit our Web site.

www.lacosta.edu/workexperience

Write sentences about the Work Experience Program at La Costa Community College.

Students are allowed to earn college credit for work experience.

> **CULTURE** NOTE
>
> Work experience programs exist in many U.S. colleges to help adult students get credit for past and present work experience.

3 Communicate

A **Work** with a partner. Read the announcement below. Ask and answer questions about the enrollment information.

> A Are students required to register early?
> B No, but students are encouraged to register early.

Do you want to enroll this fall?

You must:
- Meet with a counselor
- Sign up for a placement test
- Choose courses
- Buy books

It's a good idea to:
- Register early (space is limited)
- Find out about tutoring support
- Inquire about financial aid

B **Share** information with your classmates.

LESSON D Reading

1 Before you read

Talk with a partner. Look at the reading tip. Answer the questions.

1. Who is the story about?
2. What places are mentioned in the reading?
3. How old is their son now?

2 Read

Read the newspaper article. Listen and read again.

STUDENT TK 12
CLASS CD1 TK 16

> Scan a reading to find specific information such as names, places, and key words.

❧NEW YORK NEWS❧

An Immigrant Family's Success Story

Choi and Lili Wei left China with their baby boy in the early 1990s. They were poor field workers in their native country, and they wanted their child to have the opportunities they lacked. They arrived in New York and found a one-bedroom apartment in a poor, unstable area. They could only afford a bicycle for transportation, yet they felt fortunate to have the chance to begin a new life in the United States.

Choi and Lili faced many obstacles because they couldn't speak English and had no skills. They found night work cleaning businesses and restaurants. They saved every penny, and after six years, they were able to buy a small restaurant of their own.

They were determined to learn English, get an education, and make a good life for their son. The couple sacrificed a great deal. They never went to the movies, never ate out, and hardly ever bought anything extra. In their free time, they attended English and citizenship classes. Both of them eventually earned their GED certificates. Choi then enrolled in college while Lili worked in the restaurant.

This past spring, Choi fulfilled a lifelong dream of graduating from college. Now he is registered in a master's degree program in business beginning this fall. And what about their "baby" boy? Their son, Peter, now 21, received a scholarship to a private university, where he is working on his own dream to become an architect.

Choi and Lili are proud to be models of the "American dream." Choi has this advice for other new immigrants: "Find your passion, make a plan to succeed, and don't ever give up."

3 After you read

A Check your understanding.

1. What is Choi and Lili's native country?
2. What kind of work did they do before they came to the United States?
3. Why did they decide to come to the United States?
4. What kind of job did they find in the United States?
5. What did Choi and Lili do when they weren't working?
6. What is Peter's dream?
7. What is Choi's advice for people who want to succeed?

> **USEFUL LANGUAGE**
>
> A **synonym** is a word that has the same meaning.
>
> big - large
> nice - kind
> job - occupation

B Build your vocabulary.

1. In the reading passage, underline the words from the chart.
2. Use a dictionary or a thesaurus. Write the part of speech. Write a synonym for each word.

Word	Part of speech	Synonym
lacked	verb	missed; didn't have
unstable	adjective	insecure . changeable
fortunate	adjective	lucky
faced	verb to face =	to encounter
obstacles 障碍	noun	hindrance
determined	adjective	decide .
passion 热情	noun	warm . enthusiastic

3. Work in a small group. Write sentences with the synonyms.   *Can't lake communication*

- I think that the most important thing for a couple to get along is that they
- The weather is extremely unstable in early spring.
- Everybody needs to face a lot of people and thing every day.
- The biggest obstacles to learning a language is not speaking.
- What he's determined to do will do well.
- Her passion made every guest feel very warm.
- I'm fortunate, I met some nice people in here.

C Talk with a partner.

1. Do you believe that you are fortunate? Why or why not?
2. What are you determined to do?
3. Have you found your passion? What is it?
4. What is one obstacle you have faced?

☑ Scan a reading to find specific information such as names, places, and key words;
use a dictionary or thesaurus to identify synonyms **UNIT 2 25**

LESSON E Writing

1 Before you write

A Talk with your classmates. Answer the questions.

1. What is success? Is it only money?
2. Do you know a successful person?
3. What did the person do to become successful?
4. What was one obstacle to this person's success?

B Read the paragraph.

My Successful Cousin

My cousin, Daniel, is the most successful person I know, even though he has had many obstacles on his road to success. First of all, his parents died in an automobile accident when he was 17 years old. Daniel needed to take care of his two younger brothers, so he quit school and found a job at a local supermarket. When his brothers were in school, he worked. At night, he helped them with homework and did all the chores. Even with all his responsibilities, Daniel was a very reliable worker. His boss decided to help him go to college. It took Daniel eight years, but finally he graduated. Now Daniel plans to enroll in a business management course. If he is accepted, he hopes to open his own business someday. Daniel has a dream, and he is working hard to achieve his dream. He is my hero!

>
> Use specific details such as facts, examples, and reasons to support your topic sentence.

C Talk with a partner.

1. What are two facts given in the paragraph?
2. What are two examples given in the paragraph?
3. What is Daniel's dream?

D **Complete** the chart with Daniel's obstacles and successes.

Topic sentence: _My cousin, Daniel, is the most successful person I know,_
even though he has had many obstacles on his road to success.

Daniel's obstacles	Daniel's successes
His parents died.	He found a job in a local supermarket.

Concluding sentence: _____

E **Plan** a paragraph about a successful person you know. Use the chart to make notes on your own ideas.

Topic sentence: _____

_____'s obstacles	_____'s successes

Concluding sentence: _____

2 Write

Write a paragraph about someone you know who is successful. Include a topic sentence, examples of obstacles and successes, and a concluding sentence. Use the paragraph in Exercise 1B and the charts in Exercises 1D and 1E to help you.

3 After you write

A **Check** your writing.

	Yes	No
1. My topic sentence identifies a successful person.	☐	☐
2. I included examples of obstacles and successes.	☐	☐
3. I wrote a concluding sentence.	☐	☐

B **Share** your writing with a partner.

1. Take turns. Read your paragraph to a partner.
2. Comment on your partner's paragraph. Ask your partner a question about the paragraph. Tell your partner one thing you learned.

☑ Write a paragraph about a successful person that includes examples of obstacles and successes

LESSON F Another view

1 Life-skills reading

Location of Career Technical Education (CTE) Classes

	North Center	South Center	West Center	Downtown Center	East Center
Auto Technician	■	■	■		
Certified Nursing Assistant	■	■	■	■	■
Food Service Worker	■	■	■	■	■
Hospitality and Tourism	■				
Information Technology	■	■	■		■
Customer Service		■			
Welding	■		■		
Workplace Readiness	■	■	■	■	■

A Read the questions. Look at the chart. Fill in the answer.

1. Where are the most CTE classes offered?
   - Ⓐ Downtown Center
   - Ⓑ North Center
   - Ⓒ South Center
   - Ⓓ West Center

2. Where are the fewest CTE classes offered?
   - Ⓐ Downtown Center
   - Ⓑ North Center
   - Ⓒ South Center
   - Ⓓ East Center

3. Which program is not offered at the Downtown Center?
   - Ⓐ Food Service Worker
   - Ⓑ Workplace Readiness
   - Ⓒ Customer Service
   - Ⓓ Certified Nursing Assistant

4. Which vocational class is only offered at one site?
   - Ⓐ Certified Nursing Assistant
   - Ⓑ Hospitality and Tourism
   - Ⓒ Auto Technician
   - Ⓓ Welding

5. You want to work in a hotel. Which class is appropriate for you?
   - Ⓐ Hospitality and Tourism
   - Ⓑ Customer Service
   - Ⓒ both *a* and *b*
   - Ⓓ neither *a* nor *b*

6. You want to study computers. Which class is appropriate for you?
   - Ⓐ Auto Technician
   - Ⓑ Food Service Worker
   - Ⓒ Hospitality and Tourism
   - Ⓓ Information Technology

B Talk with a partner. Ask and answer your own questions about the chart.

2 Grammar connections: *be + supposed to* and *be + not supposed to*

Be + *supposed to* and be + *not supposed to* can show expectations about behavior.

You**'re supposed to have** your dog on a leash in a park.	You**'re not supposed to throw** your garbage on the ground.

A **Talk** with a partner. Choose one of the places in the box. Describe expectations about behavior there. Your partner guesses the place. Take turns.

a classroom	a library	a museum	a restaurant
a computer lab	a movie theater	a public bus	a swimming pool

A You're supposed to be quiet in this place. You're not supposed to use your cell phone here.
B Is it a movie theater?
A No, it isn't. You're supposed to return books on time.
B Is it a library?
A Yes, it is.

A You're not supposed to run in this place. You're supposed to pay a fee before you enter.
B Is it a museum?
A No, it isn't. You're supposed to take a shower before you get in. You're also supposed to wear a swimsuit.
B Is it a swimming pool?
A Yes, it is.

B **Share** information with the class.

> You're supposed to be quiet in a library. You're not supposed to use your cell phones, and you're supposed to return books on time.

3 Wrap up

Complete the **Self-assessment** on page 136.

☑ Scan a chart for the location of classes; contrast *be supposed to* and *be not supposed to* to show expectations about behavior **UNIT 2 29**

Review

1 Listening

Listen. Take notes on the conversation.

CLASS CD1 TK 17

1. Type of certificate	*Automotive Technology*
2. Number of required classes	
3. Total number of courses	
4. Time to complete the program	
5. Cost per course	

Talk with a partner. Check your answers.

2 Grammar

A Write. Complete the story.

A Famous Athlete

Albert Pujols _____*is considered*_____ one of the world's great baseball players. Raised
       1. considers / is considered
in the Dominican Republic, he immigrated to the United States in 1996. He demonstrated

his hitting skills _____ by batting over .500 in his first season of baseball
      2. quick / quickly
in high school. By 2001, he was playing in the major leagues for the St. Louis Cardinals. He

played so _____ that in 2006 he became the fastest player in history to
      3. good / well
reach 19 home runs in a season. In 2007 he became a citizen of the United States, getting a

_____ score on his citizenship test. Pujols _____ for
   4. perfect / perfectly   5. admires / is admired
his support of people with Down syndrome and other disabilities. A center for adults with

Down syndrome, opened in 2009, _____ for Pujols.
                6. names / is named

B Write. Look at the words that are underlined in the answers. Write the questions.

1. A _____
    B Albert Pujols grew up <u>in the Dominican Republic</u>.

2. A _____
    B He became a citizen of the United States <u>in 2007</u>.

3. A _____
    B He is admired <u>for his support of people with Down syndrome</u>.

Talk with a partner. Ask and answer the questions.

3 Pronunciation: -ed verb endings

CLASS CD1 TK 18

A **Listen** to the -ed verb endings in these sentences.

/t/
1. He has always **liked** playing number games.
2. She has **worked** as an accountant for ten years.

/d/
3. Emily has **realized** that Brenda has a good brain.
4. Naturalists are **skilled** in working with plants.

/ɪd/
5. The little boy **started** counting when he was two.
6. She is **gifted** in singing and dancing.

Listen again and repeat. Pay attention to the -ed verb endings.

CLASS CD1 TK 19

B **Listen and repeat.** Then check (✓) the correct pronunciation for each -ed verb ending.

	/t/	/d/	/ɪd/
1. Classes are **located** at various elementary schools.			
2. All students are **advised** of the school rules.			
3. An application is **required** for admission.			
4. A math test is **needed** as well.			
5. The test is **administered** once a week.			
6. The students are **expected** to pay their fees soon.			
7. Lucas hasn't **talked** with a counselor yet.			
8. But he is **finished** with all his tests.			

Talk with a partner. Compare your answers.

C **Talk** with a partner. Practice the conversations. Pay attention to the pronunciation of the -ed verb endings: /t/, /d/, or /ɪd/.

1. A Are classes offered on Saturday?
   B Yes, they are offered from 9:00 to 12:00.

2. A What are we expected to bring to class?
   B We are expected to bring a notebook, the textbook, and a pen.

3. A How did she cook?
   B She cooked very well.

4. A How did he paint?
   B He painted skillfully.

D **Write** five past tense questions. Use the following words: *administer, expect, finish, locate, provide, require* and *talk.* Then talk with a partner. Ask and answer your questions.

LESSON A
Listening

1 Before you listen

A What do you see?

B What is happening?

2 Listen

STUDENT TK 13
CLASS CD1 TK 20

A Listen and answer the questions.

1. Who are the speakers?   2. What are they talking about?

STUDENT TK 13
CLASS CD1 TK 20

B Listen again. Take notes.

Part 1	Part 2	Part 3
Reason for call: _Lan absent from class_ Action mother should take: _____	Mother's rules: _____ _____	Reason mother is upset: _____ Lan's punishment: _____ _____

3 After you listen

A Read. Complete the story.

bring (someone) up	chaperone	permitted	strict
broke (the) rules	grounded	raised	trust

> **CULTURE** NOTE
>
> When a child gets into trouble at school, the school staff calls the parents to help enforce the school rules.

Mrs. Lee received a phone message from her daughter's school saying Lan missed her 7th period class. Lan left school early to go to the mall with her friend Mary.

At the mall, Lan tells Mary that her mother is too ____strict____ . Lan thinks it's
                                                    1
because her mother wants to _____ her _____ the same way she
                                    2   2
was _____ in China. That's why Lan needs a _____ to go out on
          3   4
a date. At home, Lan and her mother have an argument. Lan is angry because

she's not _____ to go to the mall alone. She thinks her mother doesn't
                5
_____ her. Mrs. Lee is upset because Lan _____ the _____ .
      6   7   7
As a punishment, she says Lan is _____ for two weeks.
                                        8

STUDENT TK 14
CLASS CD1 TK 21

Listen and check your answers.

B Discuss. Talk with your classmates.

Do you think Lan's mother is too strict? Give reasons for your opinion.

LESSON **B** Indirect questions

1 Grammar focus: indirect *Wh-* questions

Direct *Wh-* questions	Indirect *Wh-* questions
Why is she so strict?	I wonder **why she is** so strict.
How is everything at home?	I'd like to know **how everything is** at home.
Where did you **go**?	Can you tell me **where** you **went**?
When did they **leave**?	Do you know **when** they **left**?
What did they **do**?	I don't know **what they did**.

Introductory clauses

I'd like to know . . .   Could you tell me . . . ?   Can you tell me . . . ?
I don't know . . .   I wonder . . .   Do you know . . . ?

Turn to page 143 for a grammar explanation.

> **CULTURE** NOTE
>
> Indirect questions are often more polite than direct questions. Add "please" to make the questions even more polite.

2 Practice

A Write. Change the direct questions to indirect *Wh-* questions. Circle the indirect *Wh-* questions.

1. What is the student's name?
   A Do you know _____
   (what the student's name is ?)
   B Her name is Lan.

2. What class did she miss?
   A Can you please tell me
   _____?
   B Mr. Latham's 7th period English class.

3. Why did she break the rules?
   A I would like to know
   _____.
   B I don't know why. Perhaps she was bored in class.

4. When did she and her friend leave the school?
   A I wonder _____.
   B They left after 6th period.

5. What did they do at the mall?
   A I want to know
   _____.
   B They talked and went window-shopping.

6. What was Lan's punishment?
   A Could you please tell me
   _____?
   B Her mother grounded her for two weeks.

Listen and check your answers. Then practice with a partner.

CLASS CD1 TK 22

B **Talk** with a partner about Lan's report card. Ask indirect questions.

> **A** Do you know what grade Lan got in World History?
> **B** She got a B.

School Report Card – First Semester

Student's name: Lan Suzi Lee   **Advisor: Mr. Green**

Subject	Grade	Teacher
World History	B	Lopez
Advanced English	A	Latham
Algebra	B+	Smith
P.E.	C	Chin
Chemistry	C	Hogan
Ceramics	A	Azari

Write indirect questions about Lan's report card.

Do you know what grade Lan got in World History?

3 Communicate

A **Work** with a partner. Role-play conversations between a parent and a teenager. Use indirect questions with *who*, *what*, *where*, *when*, and *why*.

> **Parent** I'd like to know why you're late.
> **Teenager** I stayed after class to talk to my math teacher.
> **Parent** OK. But next time, call me if you're going to be late. All right?

Situation 1
The teenager is two hours late coming home from school.
The parent is worried.

Situation 2
The teenager's teacher called to say the teenager was cheating on a test.
The parent is shocked.

Situation 3
The teenager's report card arrived in the mail. He or she got one A, two Bs, two Cs, and a D. Normally, the teenager gets all As and Bs. The parent is angry.

B **Perform** your role play for the class.

LESSON C Indirect questions

1 Grammar focus: indirect *Yes / No* questions

Direct *Yes / No* questions	Indirect *Yes / No* questions
Did you finish your homework?	I'd like to know **if you finished** your homework.
Is her mother strict?	I wonder **if her mother is** strict.
Will they go to college?	Could you tell me **if they will go** to college?

Turn to page 143 for a grammar explanation.

2 Practice

A Write. Complete the conversation. Use indirect *Yes / No* questions with *if*.

Son   Can I go to a party at Joe's house?

Father   Maybe. First I need to know _if you finished your homework_.
                                              1. Did you finish your homework?

Son   Yes, I finished it an hour ago.

Father   OK. Can you tell me _____?
                                   2. Will his parents be home?

Son   Yes, his parents will be there.

Father   That's good. I wonder _____.
                                   3. Do you need to take a birthday gift?

Son   No, I don't. It's not a birthday party.

Father   I wonder _____.
                             4. Are they going to serve dinner?

Son   Yes. They're going to grill chicken for us.

Father   What about your friend John?

         Do you know _____?
                            5. Is he invited to the party?

Son   Yes, I think so.

Father   Do you know _____?
                            6. Can John's parents bring you home?

Son   I'll ask them.

Listen and check your answers. Then practice with a partner.

CLASS CD1 TK 23

B **Talk** with a partner. Imagine you are a parent. Read the information you want to ask your daughter about her new friend from school. Make indirect questions using *if* or *whether*. Use a variety of introductory clauses.

> Can you tell me if she's a good student?

> I'd like to know whether she lives at home.

- is a good student
- has a job
- has nice friends
- has a good relationship with her parents

- lives alone or at home
- is polite
- drives carefully

> **USEFUL** LANGUAGE
>
> In indirect *Yes / No* questions, *whether* = *if*.

Write the parents' indirect questions.

Can you tell me if she's a good student?

3 Communicate

A **Work** in a small group. Ask and answer questions about your lives when you were teenagers. Use indirect *Yes / No* questions. Discuss the items listed below.

- relationship with parents
- grades in school
- school activities
- things you were required to do at home
- things you were permitted to do
- things you weren't permitted to do

> A I'd like to know if you got along well with your parents.
> B Yes, I did. But sometimes I argued with them.
> C I argued with my parents a lot.

B **Share** information about your classmates.

> Elena sometimes argued with her parents.
> Manny argued with his parents a lot.

LESSON **D** Reading

1 Before you read

Talk with your classmates. Answer the questions.

1. How many generations of your family are living in the United States? Which generation are you?
2. What are some of the differences between you and the other generations in your family?
3. Look at the reading tip. Look up the meaning of *barrier*, and predict what the story will be about.

> Pay attention to words that repeat in a reading. They often give you an idea of what the reading is about.

2 Read

Read the magazine article. Listen and read again.

STUDENT TK 15
CLASS CD1 TK 24

BARRIERS between GENERATIONS

In immigrant families, language differences and work schedules often create barriers to communication between the generations. Dolores Suarez, 42, and her son Diego, 16, face both kinds of barriers every day. Dolores is an immigrant from Mexico who works seven days a week as a housekeeper in a big hotel. She doesn't use much English in her job, and she has never had time to study it. Consequently, her English is limited. Her son, on the other hand, was raised in the United States. He understands Spanish, but he prefers to speak English. When his friends come over to visit, they speak only English. "They talk so fast, I can't understand what they are saying," says Dolores. To make the situation more complicated, Diego and Dolores live with Dolores's father, who speaks Nahuatl, a native language spoken in Mexico. Diego can't understand anything his grandfather says.

Dolores's work schedule is the second barrier to communication with Diego. Because she rarely has a day off, Dolores isn't able to spend much time with him. She doesn't have time to help him with his homework or attend parent-teacher conferences at his school. In 1995, when Dolores immigrated to the United States, her goal was to bring up her son with enough money to avoid the hardships her family suffered in Mexico. Her hard work has permitted Diego to have a comfortable life and a good education. But she has paid a price for this success. "Sometimes I feel like I don't know my own son," she says.

3 After you read

A Check your understanding.

1. What are the two barriers to communication between Dolores and her son?
2. Why is Dolores's English limited?
3. Which language does Diego prefer?
4. Why can't Diego communicate with his grandfather?
5. What was Dolores's goal when she came to the United States?
6. How do you think Dolores and her son could communicate better?

B Build your vocabulary.

1. In the reading passage, underline the words from the chart.
2. Use a dictionary. Fill in the chart with the missing word forms.

Noun	Verb	Adjective
immigrant	*immigrate*	*immigrant*
differences		
	create	
communication		
education		
success		

3. Complete the sentences. Write the correct form of the word from Exercise B2.

   a. My family decided to _____ to the United States because there was a war in my country.

   b. Parents and teenagers almost always _____ in the kind of music they prefer.

   c. Shosha paints beautiful and unusual oil paintings. She's very

      _____ .

   d. Debra's son isn't very _____ . It's hard to know what he's thinking.

   e. It's a parent's responsibility to _____ children about right and wrong behavior.

   f. You need two things to be _____ in life: motivation and luck.

C Talk with a partner.

1. What are some ways that you and your parents are different?
2. How can parents help children be more creative?
3. How can people communicate if they don't speak the same language?
4. Is it necessary to go to school to be an educated person? Explain your answer.

LESSON **E** Writing

1 Before you write

A Talk with a partner. What are some differences between you and your parents or you and your children? Write your information on the charts.

Me	My parents	Me	My children
like salads and sandwiches	like lamb and rice	play cards	play video games

B Read the paragraph.

> Transitions like *for example* and *on the other hand* show the relationship between sentences or ideas in a paragraph.

Different Eating Habits

One difference between my parents and me is that we don't have the same eating habits. My family is Iranian, but I was brought up in the United States. Since most of my friends are American, I enjoy eating "American style." For example, I like to eat salads and sandwiches instead of meat and rice. Because of my job, I don't have time to cook, so I like fast food. I also love to eat in restaurants. On the other hand, my parents still eat like they did back home. They eat rice with every meal, and they eat a lot of lamb and vegetables. They don't like to eat in restaurants because my father thinks my mother is the best cook in the world. Actually, I agree with him. I still love my mother's cooking even though our eating habits are different.

C Work with a partner. Complete the outline of the model paragraph.

Topic sentence: *One difference between my parents and me is that we don't have the same eating habits.*

1 Me: *I enjoy eating "American style."*
  a. Example: *I like to eat salads and sandwiches.*
  b. Example: *I don't eat a lot of meat and rice.*
  c. Example: *I like fast food.*

Transition: *On the other hand*

2 My parents: _____

  a. Example: _____

  b. Example: _____

  c. Example: _____

D Plan a paragraph about a difference between you and your parents or you and your children. Include at least three examples to support your main idea. Make an outline. Use your own paper.

■ 2 Write

Write a paragraph about a difference between you and your parents or you and your children. Include a topic sentence that identifies the difference. Give examples to support the main idea, and use a transition between the two parts of your paragraph. Use the paragraph in Exercise 1B and the outlines in Exercises 1C and 1D to help you.

■ 3 After you write

A Check your writing.

	Yes	No
1. My topic sentence states the difference between my parents and me or my children and me.	☐	☐
2. I gave examples to support the main idea.	☐	☐
3. I used a transition between the two parts of my paragraph.	☐	☐

B Share your writing with a partner.

1. Take turns. Read your paragraph to a partner.
2. Comment on your partner's paragraph. Ask your partner a question about the paragraph. Tell your partner one thing you learned.

LESSON F Another view

1 Life-skills reading

U.S. Census Bureau

2010 American Community Survey: Households and Families
Total number of households: 114,567,419

Subject	Married couple family households	Female householder, no spouse present	Male householder, no spouse present	Non-family household
Total number of households	55,704,781 49%	14,998,476 13%	5,385,788 4%	38,478,374 34%
Average family size	3.25	3.22	3.03	X
Households with one or more children under 18	44%	66.7%	56.6%	.9%
Households with one or more people 60+ years old	34.1%	23.8%	25%	39.5%

source: U.S. Census Bureau - Households and Families

A Read the questions. Look at the survey results. Fill in the answer.

1. Of the four types of households in the United States in 2010, which type is the least common?

    Ⓐ married couple family households

    Ⓑ female householder, no spouse present

    Ⓒ male householder, no spouse present

    Ⓓ non-family household

2. What percentage of households are non-family households?

    Ⓐ 4%

    Ⓑ 13%

    Ⓒ 34%

    Ⓓ 49%

3. According to the survey, which family type has the largest percent of households with one or more children under 18?

    Ⓐ households led by females with no spouse present

    Ⓑ non-family households

    Ⓒ married couple family households

    Ⓓ households led by males with no spouse present

4. Which of the following statements is not true about households led by males with no spouse present?

    Ⓐ More than half of them have one or more children under 18 living there.

    Ⓑ There are over 50,000,000 of them.

    Ⓒ 1/4 of them have one or more people 60+ years old living there.

    Ⓓ The average family size is 3.03.

B Talk with a partner. What do you think about these survey results? Does anything surprise you?

2 Grammar connections: *say* and *tell* with reported speech

Direct Speech	Reported Speech
"I have a cat."	Tatiana **said (that)** she has a cat. She **told me (that)** she has a cat. She **told Andrew (that)** she has a cat.

A **Work** in a small group. One person asks a question from the list. One person answers. One person reports the answer with *say*. One person reports the answer with *tell*. Take turns.

> **A** Who do you live with?
> **B** I live with my cousin.
> **C** She said that she lives with her cousin.
> **D** She told him that she lives with her cousin.

Questions:

1. Who do you live with?
2. Where do you live?
3. What language do you speak at home?
4. What kind of car do you drive?
5. How many brothers and sisters do you have?
6. Do you have children? How many?
7. What kinds of foods does your family eat?
8. What is your favorite food?
9. What do you do for fun?
10. Why do you study English?
11. How often are you absent from class?
12. How often are you late to class?
13. What school subjects do you like?
14. Do you have a job? Where do you work?

B **Share** information about your classmates.

> Laura told Andrew that she lives with her cousin. She told him she lives downtown. She said that she speaks Spanish at home.

3 Wrap up

Complete the **Self-assessment** on page 137.

LESSON A
Listening

1 Before you listen

A What do you see?

B What is happening?

Unit Goals	Recognize causes of stress
	Explain strategies for coping with stress
	Recognize the impact of stress on work

2 Listen

A **Listen** and answer the questions.

1. Who are the speakers?   2. What are they talking about?

B **Listen again.** Complete the chart.

Sara's symptoms	Mike's advice
1. *can't sleep*	4. _____
2. _____	5. _____
3. _____	6. _____

3 After you listen

A **Read.** Complete the story.

anxiety	calm down	cope with	stressed out
breathing	concentrate	meditation	tense

> Mike is driving Sara to the Department of Motor Vehicles (DMV) to take her driving test. He notices that she's very _____tense_____ . Sara says she's
> 1
> _____ because she was late to work again. She's worried that her boss
> 2
> will fire her if she's late one more time. She's so afraid of losing her job that she
> can't eat, she can't sleep, and she can't _____ . Mike says that she has to
> 3
> _____ if she wants to pass her driving test. He suggests three techniques
> 4
> to help her _____ her _____ . One is deep _____ .
> 5   6   7
> The second one is thinking positive thoughts, and the third one is _____ .
> 8

Listen and check your answers.

B **Discuss.** Talk with your classmates.

1. Do you ever feel stressed out? What makes you feel stressed out?
2. What helps you when you feel stressed out?

LESSON **B** Modals

1 Grammar focus: *should, shouldn't, have to, don't have to*

Advisable = good idea	Not advisable = bad idea
Sara **should learn** how to meditate.	She **shouldn't get** stressed out.

Necessary	Not necessary
Sara **has to take** public transportation because she doesn't have a car.	She **doesn't have to take** her driving test today. She can take it next week.

Turn to page 143 for a complete grammar chart and explanation.

2 Practice

A Write. Complete the story. Use *should*, *shouldn't*, *have to*, and *don't have to*.

Ana and Bill just got engaged, and they are planning to get married in four weeks. Because the wedding is so soon, they are feeling a lot of pressure. Ana's mother wants a big wedding, but Ana and Bill don't. Because they are paying for the wedding themselves, they believe they ____*should*____ do what they
                                                    1
want. Another pressure is all the things Ana and Bill

_____ do before the wedding. For example, Ana _____ buy a
         2   3
dress, choose her bridesmaids, and send out the invitations. Bill _____
                                                                            4
plan the reception and order the food. Most importantly, they _____
                                                                        5
decide where the wedding will be. Ana wants to get married outdoors, but Bill thinks

they _____ plan an outdoor wedding because it might rain. Now Bill has
          6
a different idea. He realizes that they _____ get married so soon. Maybe
                                                  7
they _____ postpone the wedding by a few months. That way, they
          8
_____ feel so much pressure.
      9

 Listen and check your answers.

CLASS CD1 TK 27

B Talk with a partner. Make sentences about the people in the pictures. Use *should, shouldn't, ought to, have to,* and *don't have to.* Use the items from the box in your sentences.

Carmela and Hugo ought to try to meet new people.

Chul and Sun-mi have to find a new place to live.

Carmela and Hugo
• just got married
• just moved to a new town

Chul and Sun-mi
• just had a baby
• live in a studio apartment

Kevin
• just started his first job
• still lives with his parents

try to meet new people	ask lots of questions
call parents about every problem	find a new place to live
learn how to manage money	follow their (his) parents' advice
try to do everything perfectly	make decisions by themselves (himself)
buy baby furniture	be responsible
meet the neighbors	volunteer at a local organization

Write sentences about the people in the pictures.

Carmela and Hugo ought to try to meet new people.

3 Communicate

A Work in a small group. Discuss the following situations, and give advice. Use *should, shouldn't, ought to, have to,* and *don't have to.*

They have to buy furniture.

They should check the newspaper for furniture sales.

1. The Wong family just bought a house. The house has no furniture at all. Also, it is far from Mr. Wong's job, and the family doesn't have a car.
2. Etsuko and Hiro immigrated to the United States. They are anxious because there are so many things to do. They don't have a big enough place to live, they aren't enrolled in English classes, and their children aren't registered for school.
3. Boris is very nervous about his new job. He doesn't know anyone at the company yet, and he doesn't know his duties yet, either. His boss is a woman. He has never worked for a woman before.

B Share your group's advice with your classmates.

LESSON C Past modals

1 Grammar focus: *should have* and *shouldn't have*

Regret in the past	Advice in the past
I don't like my new job.	Robert is late to work.
I **should have kept** my old job.	He **should have left** the house earlier.
I **shouldn't have changed** jobs.	He **shouldn't have read** the newspaper before work.

Turn to page 144 for a complete grammar chart and explanation.
Turn to page 149 for a list of past participles.

2 Practice

A Write. Read about Imelda. Write sentences with *should have* and *shouldn't have*.

Imelda left the Philippines last year and immigrated to the United States. None of her family came with her. She got homesick and depressed.

1. She didn't talk to anyone about her problems.
   She should have talked to someone about her problems.

2. She didn't go out with friends.
   _____

3. She stayed home alone all the time.
   _____

4. She didn't make new friends.
   _____

5. She didn't exercise.
   _____

6. She didn't eat regular, balanced meals.
   _____

7. She ate lots of junk food.
   _____

8. She slept so much.
   _____

9. She didn't call her family.
   _____

Listen and check your answers.

B **Talk** with a partner. Look at the pictures. What should Nikolai and his boss have done differently? Use *shouldn't have*.

> Nikolai shouldn't have overslept.

oversleep

forget (his) briefcase

arrive late

criticize (someone) in public

leave the meeting

lose (their) temper

Write sentences about what Nikolai and his boss should have done instead.

Nikolai should have gotten up on time.

3 Communicate

A **Work** in a small group. Think about a past situation in your life that didn't go well. Take turns asking and answering questions about it.

1. What was the situation?
2. What did you do that you shouldn't have?
3. What didn't you do that you should have?

B **Share** information about your classmates.

LESSON **D** Reading

1 Before you read

Talk with your classmates. Answer the questions.

1. When you are in a stressful situation, what happens to your body?
2. Read the **boldfaced** questions (section heads) in the article. Talk with a partner. Share your answers to these questions before you read the article.

2 Read

Read the magazine article. Listen and read again.

STUDENT TK 18
CLASS CD1 TK 29

> Before you read an article, read the title and section heads. Relate them to your own background and experience.

STRESS: What You Ought to Know

What is stress?

Stress is our reaction to changing events in our lives. The reactions can be mental – what we think or feel about the changes – and physical – how our body reacts to the changes.

What causes stress?

Stress often comes when there are too many changes in our lives. The changes can be positive, like having a baby or getting a better job, or they can be negative, such as an illness or a divorce. Some stress is healthy. It motivates us to push forward. But too much stress over time can make us sick.

What are the signs of stress?

There are both physical and emotional signs of stress. Physical signs may include tight muscles, elevated blood pressure, grinding your teeth, trouble sleeping, an upset stomach, and back pain. Common emotional symptoms are anxiety, nervousness, depression, trouble concentrating, and nightmares.

How can you manage stress?

To prevent stress, you should eat right and exercise regularly. When you know there will be a stressful event in your day – such as a test, a business meeting, or an encounter with someone you don't get along with – it is really important to eat a healthy breakfast and to limit coffee and sugar.

When you find yourself in a stressful situation, stay calm. Take a few deep breaths to help you relax. Roll your shoulders or stretch to loosen any tight muscles. And take time to think before you speak. You don't want to say something you will regret later!

3 After you read

A Check your understanding.

1. What are some physical signs of stress?
2. What are some emotional signs of stress?
3. What should you eat when you know there will be a stressful event in your life? What foods should you avoid?
4. Do you have a favorite exercise that you do to reduce stress? If so, what is it?
5. Think of a time when there were many changes in your life. Were the changes positive or negative? How did you feel? How did your body react?

B Build your vocabulary.

1. English uses suffixes to change the part of speech of a word. Underline words in the reading that end with the suffixes in the left column.

2. Complete the chart. Use a dictionary if necessary.

Suffix	Example	Part of speech	Main word	Part of speech
-ful	*stressful*	*adj*	*stress*	*noun*
-en				
-ly				
-ness				
-ion				

3. Complete the sentences. Write the correct form of the word from Exercise B2.

a. My shirt collar is too tight. I need to _____*loosen*_____ it.
b. When you are sick, you should stay home. You do not want to give your _____ to others.
c. You should limit coffee and sugar when you are going to be in a _____ situation.
d. One emotional symptom of stress is depression. Another is _____ .
e. She is worried about her weight, so she exercises _____ .
f. Tight muscles are an example of a physical _____ to stress.

C Talk with a partner.

1. What's a stressful situation you've been in recently?
2. Why is it important to exercise regularly?
3. What are some physical habits that can show nervousness?
4. Is it a good idea to take medicine for depression? Why or why not?
5. Do your muscles often get tight? How do you loosen them?

☑ Relate the title and section heads to your own background and experience; recognize suffixes that change part of speech **UNIT 4 51**

LESSON E Writing

1 Before you write

A **Talk** with a partner. Look at the pictures. Answer the questions.

1. How do the people in the pictures cope with stress?
2. What are some healthy ways of coping with stress?
3. What are some unhealthy ways of coping with stress?
4. What makes you feel stressed?

B **Read** the paragraph.

How I Cope with Stress

When I feel stressed, I like to curl up with my cat, listen to classical music, and read an interesting book. Stroking my cat's soft fur helps my body relax, and soon I feel less tense. The sound of classical music with piano and string instruments shuts out the noises around me and reduces my anxiety. I like to listen with my eyes closed until my muscles start to relax. Then I open my eyes and pick up a book. I usually choose stories about people and the difficult events in their lives because they help me forget about all the stressful things I have to do in my own life.

> One way to organize details in a paragraph is to write about cause and effect.
>
> *I like to listen with my eyes closed* (cause) *until my muscles start to relax* (effect).

C Work with a partner. Complete the outline of the model paragraph.

Topic sentence: When I feel stressed, _____

_____

Ways of reducing stress:

cause: *stroke my cat's fur* _____ → effect: *body relaxes, feel less tense* _____

cause: _____ → effect: _____

cause: _____ → effect: _____

D Plan a paragraph about how you cope with stress. Use the outline to make notes on your ideas.

Topic sentence: When I feel stressed, _____

_____

_____ .

Ways of reducing stress:

cause: _____ → effect: _____

cause: _____ → effect: _____

cause: _____ → effect: _____

2 Write

Write a paragraph about how you cope with stress. Write about at least three ways of reducing stress (causes) and the effect of each. Use details to describe each effect. Use the paragraph in Exercise 1B and the outlines in Exercises 1C and 1D to help you.

3 After you write

A Check your writing.

	Yes	No
1. My topic sentence identifies three ways of reducing stress.	☐	☐
2. For each cause, I described an effect.	☐	☐
3. I used details to describe each effect.	☐	☐

B Share your writing with a partner.

1. Take turns. Read your paragraph to a partner.
2. Comment on your partner's paragraph. Ask your partner a question about the paragraph. Tell your partner one thing you learned.

LESSON **F** Another view

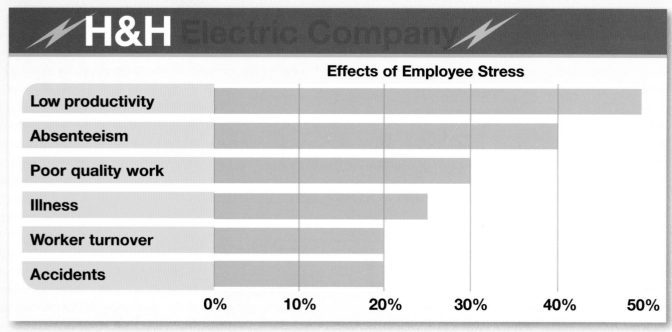

H&H Electric Company

Effects of Employee Stress

Low productivity
Absenteeism
Poor quality work
Illness
Worker turnover
Accidents

0%   10%   20%   30%   40%   50%

A Read the questions. Look at the bar graph. Fill in the answer.

1. This chart is about _____.
   - (A) how stress affects employees
   - (B) how stress affects a business
   - (C) both *a* and *b*
   - (D) neither *a* nor *b*

2. Employee stress is the cause of _____.
   - (A) 30 percent of poor quality work
   - (B) 20 percent of worker turnover
   - (C) both *a* and *b*
   - (D) neither *a* nor *b*

3. Employee stress contributes to worker turnover less than it contributes to _____.
   - (A) low productivity
   - (B) poor work quality
   - (C) illness
   - (D) all of the above

4. Employee stress affects accidents as much as it affects _____.
   - (A) absenteeism
   - (B) worker turnover
   - (C) both *a* and *b*
   - (D) neither *a* nor *b*

5. Employee stress affects _____ the most.
   - (A) productivity
   - (B) work quality
   - (C) illness
   - (D) absenteeism

6. The chart does not show how stress affects _____.
   - (A) absenteeism
   - (B) illness
   - (C) tardiness
   - (D) accidents

B Talk with your classmates. Should employers do something to relieve stress in the workplace? Why or why not? What could they do?

2 Grammar connections: *must* and *may / might*

Use *must* when you are pretty sure (80%).	Use *may* and *might* when you are less sure (50% or less).
Situation: Sergio works 60 hours a week.	
He **must be** tired. He **must not have** time to relax.	He **might be** tired. He **may be** tired. He **might not have** time to relax. He **may not have** time to relax.

A **Work** in a small group. Look at the results of the stress test. Say what you think about the people. Use *may*, *might*, and *must* in your answers.

> A Tina must be tired during the day. She only sleeps five hours a night.
> B You know, she might not need a lot of sleep. She still works a lot and is able to exercise every day.
> C In fact, she exercises a lot, and she doesn't eat much. She may be worried about her weight.

Stress Test

Name	Tina	Sergio	Larisa
1. How many meals do you eat a day?	One	Five	Three
2. Do you eat balanced meals?	No	No	Yes
3. How many cups of coffee do you drink a day?	Five	Two	None
4. How many hours do you sleep at night?	Five	Six	Nine
5. How often do you exercise?	Once a day	Never	Once a week
6. Do you worry about other people?	Yes	No	Yes
7. How often do you get angry?	Never	Every day	Rarely
8. Do you take time each day for yourself?	No	No	Yes
9. How often do you do fun things with friends or family?	Rarely	Once a week	Every day
10. How many hours a week are you at work or school?	45	60	25

B **Share** your group's ideas with the class.

> Most of us think that Tina must be tired a lot, although some of us think she might not need a lot of sleep. She may be . . .

3 Wrap up

Complete the **Self-assessment** on page 137.

Review

CLASS CD1 TK 30

Listen to the phone conversation. Take notes.

Yesenia's symptoms	Sue's suggestions
1. *tense*	4.
2.	5.
3.	6.

Talk with a partner. Check your answers.

2 Grammar

A Write. Complete the story. Use indirect questions.

Ann's Night Out

Ann is 16 years old. It's midnight, and she isn't home yet. She went out with

her friend Liz. Ann's mom doesn't know ___*where they went*___ . She wonders
                                          1. Where did they go?

_____ . Ann's mother wants to call Liz's house, but she
    2. Are Ann and Liz safe?

doesn't know _____ . Ann's father is worried, too. He wonders
                3. What is the phone number?

_____ . Then he hears a sound downstairs. For a minute, he
    4. Can he find them?

doesn't know _____ . It's Ann! Her father says, "We had no
                5. Who is it?

idea _____ , but we're glad you're home."
        6. Where were you?

B Write. Look at the words that are underlined in the answers. Write the questions.

1. A _____

   B Ann should have been home <u>at 11:00</u>.

2. A _____

   B She should have called <u>her parents</u>.

3. A _____

   B Ann's parents should <u>ground her</u>.

Talk with a partner. Ask and answer the questions.

3 Pronunciation: intonation in *Wh-* questions

CLASS CD1 TK 31

A **Listen** to the intonation in these *Wh-* questions.

Direct question

Where did he go?

Indirect question

Can you tell me where he went?

Listen again and repeat. Pay attention to the intonation.

CLASS CD1 TK 32

B **Listen and repeat.** Then draw arrows to show rising or falling intonation in the questions.

1. A What does Ann do to reduce stress?
   B She listens to music.

2. A Why are you so tense?
   B I have my driver's test today.

3. A Do you know what Rodolfo does to calm down?
   B He walks or jogs.

4. A When did Ivan miss his class?
   B He missed his class on Tuesday.

5. A Can you tell me where Andy lives?
   B He lives on East Fifth Street.

6. A Do you know why they're always late?
   B No, I don't know.

Talk with a partner. Compare your answers.

C **Talk** with a partner. Ask and answer the questions. Use the correct intonation.

1. What is one thing you should have done today or yesterday?
2. What is a common punishment for teenagers when they come home late?
3. What were your favorite things to do when you were growing up?
4. Can you tell me what you do to reduce stress?
5. Do you know why it's important to exercise regularly?
6. Do you know if meditation is difficult to do?

D **Write** five questions. Make at least three indirect questions. Ask your partner.

Can you tell me how you cope with stressful situations?

1. _____
2. _____
3. _____
4. _____
5. _____

Talk with a partner. Ask and answer the questions.

LESSON **A**
Listening

1 Before you listen

A What do you see?

B What is happening?

Unit Goals	Describe benefits of volunteering
	Describe someone who made a difference
	Identify information in advertisements for volunteer positions

UNIT 5

2 Listen

STUDENT TK 19
CLASS CD1 TK 33

A Listen and answer the questions.

1. Who are the speakers?   2. What are they talking about?

STUDENT TK 19
CLASS CD1 TK 33

B Listen again. Complete the chart.

Almaz's responsibilities at the library	Volunteer responsibilities at Quiet Palms
1. *worked with adults learning to read*	4.
2.	5.
3.	6.

3 After you listen

A Read. Complete the story.

can't wait	compassionate	orientation	residents
commitment	coordinator	patient	worthwhile

Last summer, Almaz volunteered at the public library downtown. She liked

working with the older people because she felt that she was doing something

___worthwhile___. Today, she is meeting with Steve, the volunteer _____ at
    1   2

Quiet Palms, a nursing home. She wants to volunteer there to find out if she likes

working in the health-care field. Steve tells her about some of her responsibilities

at Quiet Palms. He says it's very important for volunteers to be _____ and
                                                             3

_____ when they are working with the _____. He asks Almaz to
    4   5

make a _____ to volunteer at least three hours per week. Almaz agrees to
          6

attend an _____. She says she _____ to start volunteering.
            7   8

CULTURE NOTE

A *nursing home* is a place where elderly people live when their families can't take care of them.

STUDENT TK 20
CLASS CD1 TK 34

Listen and check your answers.

B Talk with your classmates.

What are some places in your community to volunteer? What are some benefits of volunteering?

LESSON B Time clauses

1 Grammar focus: clauses with *until* and *as soon as*

***until* = up to a particular time**

> Almaz **will stay** with Mr. Shamash **until** he **finishes** his lunch.
> **Until** Mr. Shamash **finishes** his lunch, Almaz **will stay** with him.

***as soon as* = right after**

> Almaz **will leave** Quiet Palms **as soon as** Mr. Shamash **finishes** his lunch.
> **As soon as** Mr. Shamash **finishes** his lunch, Almaz **will leave** Quiet Palms.

Turn to page 144 for a grammar explanation.

USEFUL LANGUAGE

The part of the sentence that begins with *until* or *as soon as* is a time clause. It can be the first half or the second half of the sentence.

2 Practice

A Write. Complete the sentences with *until* or *as soon as*. Circle the time clause.

1. A Mr. Shamash is in pain. When will he start to feel better?
   B He'll feel better ⟨*as soon as* he takes his medication.⟩

2. A How long will Mr. Shamash stay at Quiet Palms?
   B He'll stay _____ his broken hip heals.

3. A When can Mr. Shamash begin exercising again?
   B _____ Mr. Shamash feels stronger, he can start doing moderate exercise.

4. A When does Mr. Shamash get ready for his walk?
   B He gets ready _____ Almaz arrives.

5. A How long will Mr. Shamash and Almaz play cards?
   B They'll play cards _____ it is time for lunch.

6. A How long will Almaz stay with Mr. Shamash?
   B She'll stay _____ his family arrives to visit him.

7. A When is Mr. Shamash going to go to sleep?
   B _____ his visitors leave, he'll take his medicine and go to sleep.

CLASS CD1 TK 35

Listen and check your answers. Then practice with a partner.

B **Talk** with a partner. Discuss Charles's volunteer activities at a nursing home. Use *as soon as* or *until*.

As soon as Charles arrives at work, he puts on his name tag.

Charles doesn't put on his name tag until he arrives at work.

1. arrive / put on name tag

2. walk with Mrs. Halliday / time to deliver mail

3. read to Mrs. Halliday / lunchtime

4. stop reading / lunch is delivered

5. talk to Mrs. Halliday / finish eating

6. go home / finish playing a game with Mrs. Halliday

Write sentences about Charles's volunteer activities.

As soon as Charles arrives at work, he puts on his name tag.

3 Communicate

A **Choose** one time when you helped someone or volunteered. Make a list of your activities. Use Exercise 2B to help you.

B **Work** with a partner. Ask questions about each other's activities. Use *as soon as* and *until*.

A I volunteered at an animal shelter.
B What did you do as soon as you arrived?
A I checked the board for my duties.
B How late did you stay?
A I stayed until the shelter closed for the day.

C **Share** information about your partner.

LESSON C Verb tense contrast

1 Grammar focus: repeated actions in the present and past

		Number of times	Time expressions
Present	This year, Sana **volunteers** at the homeless shelter This year, Sana **is volunteering** at the homeless shelter	once twice three times several times many times	a week. each month.
Past	Sana **volunteered** at the homeless shelter		last year. two years ago. when she was 12.
Present perfect	Sana **has volunteered** at the homeless shelter		so far. recently. in her life.

Turn to page 144 for a complete grammar chart and explanation.

2 Practice

A Write. Complete the story with the present, present perfect, or past forms of the verbs.

Sharing with Sally

Sally Sutherland created "Sharing with Sally," a volunteer organization that helps seniors stay connected with the outside world. The organization

has delivered over 5,000 dinners to seniors
    1. deliver

so far. Sharing with Sally _____ six
                     2. begin

years ago. Several times a week, Sally and her volunteers _____ meals,
                                                      3. deliver

_____ to seniors on the phone, and _____ the ones who can't leave
    4. talk   5. visit

their homes. Over 200 people volunteer at Sharing with Sally. Jake, a college student,

_____ all last year. He _____ elderly people on the phone once a
    6. volunteer   7. call

week and _____ to each person. He said it was a very valuable experience.
        8. talk

Betsy, a 35-year-old mother of two, _____ for two years so far and loves it.
                                  9. volunteer

Listen and check your answers.

B **Talk** with a partner. Make sentences about Betsy's volunteer experience. Include the number of times and time expressions.

> **A** Betsy visited seniors at their homes 30 times last year.
> **B** She's also visited them 15 times so far this year.

USEFUL LANGUAGE

she's visited = she has visited

Activity	Number of times last year	Number of times this year
Visit seniors at their homes	30	15
Deliver meals	25	10
Call seniors on the phone	45	25
Help Sally put meals in the truck	5	1
Take her children with her to the seniors' homes	10	3

Write sentences about Betsy's activities.

Betsy visited seniors at their homes 30 times last year.

3 Communicate

A **Make** a list of your experiences volunteering or helping people.

Last year	This year
took my grandmother to the hairdresser	*volunteer at a homeless shelter*

B **Work** with a partner. Share your lists. Ask questions about your partner's activities. Use *How often . . . ?* or *How many times . . . ?*

> How often did you take your grandmother to the hairdresser last year?
>> Every week.

> How often do you volunteer at a homeless shelter?
>> Several times a year.

> How many times have you volunteered at the homeless shelter so far this year?
>> Three times.

C **Share** information about your partner.

☑ Use correct verb tense to show repeated actions in the present and past **UNIT 5** **63**

LESSON **D** Reading

1 Before you read

Talk with your classmates. Answer the questions.

1. Look at the picture. What is unusual about it?
2. Read the title. What do you think the story will be about?

2 Read

Read the newspaper article. Listen and read again.

STUDENT TK 21
CLASS CD1 TK 37

> Use titles and pictures to help
> predict what a reading is about.

RUNNING WITH ROPES

Imagine running with your eyes closed. How do you feel? Insecure? Afraid? Justin Andrews knows these feelings very well. Justin is a former long-distance runner who lost his vision because of a grave illness. For the past six months, he has been running twice a week with the help of volunteer runners at Running with Ropes, an organization that assists blind and visually impaired runners. "Running with Ropes has changed my life," Justin says. "Until I heard about it, I thought I'd never run outside again."

Volunteers at Running with Ropes make a commitment to volunteer two to four hours a week. Scott Liponi, one of the running volunteers, explains what they do. "We use ropes to join ourselves to the blind runners and guide them around and over obstacles, such as holes in the road and other runners." Scott has learned how to keep the rope loose so the blind runner has more freedom. He deeply respects the blind runners' tenacity. "They are incredibly determined," he says. "It doesn't matter if it's hot, raining, or snowing – they are going to run." Scott says it is gratifying to share in the joy of the runners and to feel that they trust him. "The four hours I spend at Running with Ropes are the most rewarding part of my week," he says. "It's really a worthwhile commitment."

3 After you read

A Check your understanding.

1. Who is Justin Andrews? What happened to him?
2. What is Running with Ropes?
3. How is Justin able to run?
4. Who is Scott Liponi?
5. How does Scott feel about his volunteer commitment?

> When you see a new word, look at the words around it to guess if the meaning is positive or negative.
>
> *He lost his vision because of a grave illness.*
>
> You can guess that *grave* has a negative meaning because loss of vision and illness are both negative events.

B Build your vocabulary.

1. Look at the reading tip above. Then, in the reading passage, underline the words from the chart. Decide if their meanings are positive or negative. Fill in the clues that helped you guess.

Word	Positive	Negative	Clue
1. grave		✓	*He lost his vision because of an illness.*
2. insecure			
3. impaired			
4. freedom			
5. tenacity			
6. gratifying			
7. rewarding			

2. Work with your classmates. Write four more words from the reading that have positive or negative meanings. Indicate if their meanings are positive or negative. Fill in the clues that helped you guess.

Word	Positive	Negative	Clue
a.			
b.			
c.			
d.			

C Talk with a partner.

1. When do you feel most insecure?
2. Tell about something that takes tenacity.
3. Describe a gratifying experience.
4. What do visually impaired people use to help them? What about hearing-impaired people?

☑ Use pictures and titles to predict what a reading is about; use context clues to decide if a word has a positive or negative meaning

LESSON E Writing

1 Before you write

A Talk with your classmates. Look at the picture. Answer the questions.

1. Who are the people in the picture? Where are they? What are they doing?
2. Do you think the young woman is doing something important? Why or why not?

B Read the paragraph.

Story Lady

My friend Vivianne is one of the most compassionate people I have ever met. After college, she wanted to do something truly worthwhile, so she spent a year working as a literacy volunteer in northeastern Brazil. At the time, this area didn't have any libraries, so Vivianne traveled to different schools in a mobile library van. As soon as she arrived at a school, the children would run outside and shout, "Story Lady! Story Lady!" Then everyone went inside, sat down, and listened quietly while she read them a story. Vivianne made a huge difference in these children's lives. She introduced them to literature and taught them to love reading. Today, she still gets letters from children who remember her generosity and kindness.

> Make your writing more interesting by including specific details that answer the questions *who, what, where, when, why,* and *how.*

C **Work** with a partner. Write the words *who, what, where, when, why,* or *how* next to the details from the paragraph.

1. _____*who*_____ my friend Vivianne
2. _____ after college
3. _____ a literacy volunteer
4. _____ northeastern Brazil
5. _____ because the area didn't have any libraries
6. _____ in a mobile library van
7. _____ read stories to the children
8. _____ taught the children to love reading

D **Plan** a paragraph about someone you know who made a difference. Use the chart to make notes.

Who made a difference?	
What did he or she do?	
Where did it happen?	
When did it happen?	
Why did this person do it?	

2 Write

Write a paragraph about someone you know who made a difference in your life or someone else's life. Include specific details that answer *Wh-* questions. Use the paragraph in Exercise 1B and the chart in Exercise 1D to help you.

3 After you write

A **Check** your writing.

	Yes	No
1. My topic sentence names the person who made a difference.	☐	☐
2. I included specific details in my paragraph.	☐	☐
3. The details in my paragraph answer *Wh-* questions.	☐	☐

B **Share** your writing with a partner.

1. Take turns. Read your paragraph to a partner.
2. Comment on your partner's paragraph. Ask your partner a question about the paragraph. Tell your partner one thing you learned.

LESSON F Another view

1 Life-skills reading

Want to get involved?
Volunteer opportunities are listed every Wednesday.

HOME   ABOUT US   CONTACT US

1. Health
Agency: San Antonio Meals for Seniors
Need: Volunteers to drive meals to seniors' homes
Contact: Jim Jefferies, 555-2324

Site: Downtown area
Time commitment: 3 hours per week

2. Literacy
Agency: San Antonio Literacy Foundation
Need: Volunteers to tutor basic reading, writing, and math skills to adults
Contact: 555-3131

Site: Around the city
Time commitment: 4 hours per week, 3-month commitment, plus 12 hours training

3. Animals
Agency: "Make People Smile" Animal Therapy
Need: Volunteers and their pets to visit hospitals and nursing homes
Contact: Judy, jsmith@mpsat.org

Site: Throughout the city
Time commitment: 4 hours per month

4. General Administration
Agency: San Antonio Zoo
Need: Volunteers to help with mailings and other office jobs; assist various departments, including administration, marketing, and membership
Contact: Tina de la Peña, 555-5432

Site: Zoo's administration building
Time commitment: Flexible

A **Read** the questions. Look at the advertisements for volunteer positions. Fill in the answer.

1. Which volunteer position requires the biggest time commitment?
   - Ⓐ 1
   - Ⓑ 2
   - Ⓒ 3
   - Ⓓ 4

2. Which ad does not give a phone number?
   - Ⓐ 1
   - Ⓑ 2
   - Ⓒ 3
   - Ⓓ 4

3. Which position requires math skills?
   - Ⓐ 1
   - Ⓑ 2
   - Ⓒ 3
   - Ⓓ none of the positions

4. Which position requires office skills?
   - Ⓐ 1
   - Ⓑ 2
   - Ⓒ 3
   - Ⓓ 4

5. Which position requires a driver's license?
   - Ⓐ 1
   - Ⓑ 2
   - Ⓒ 3
   - Ⓓ 4

6. Which position requires some training?
   - Ⓐ 1
   - Ⓑ 2
   - Ⓒ 3
   - Ⓓ none of the positions

B **Talk** with your classmates. Discuss the ads. Which ones are interesting to you? Why?

2 Grammar connections: *used to* and *be used to*

Use *used to* + verb for past situations that are not true now.	Use *be used to* + gerund or noun for things a person is accustomed to.
I **used to** <u>eat</u> a lot of sandwiches as a child. I **didn't use to** <u>eat</u> meat.	I **am used to** <u>eating</u> fish for dinner. I **am not used to** <u>eating</u> dessert. Katia **is used to** <u>American food</u>.
What **did** you **use to** <u>eat</u> as a child?	What **are** you **used to** <u>eating</u> for dinner?

A **Work** in a small group. Play the game. Write your name on a small piece of paper. Flip a coin to move your paper. Then tell your group your answer to the question in the square. Use *used to* or *be used to* in your answer. Take turns.

 = 1 space

 = 2 spaces

> This says, "What did you use to do for fun as a child?" Well, I used to play in the park with my sister. We had a lot of fun.

Start here →	What did you use to do for fun as a child? →	How often are you used to going to the supermarket? →	How did you use to get to school as a child?
Who are you used to helping in your family? ←	What kind of weather are you used to? ←	How did you use to wear your hair as a child? ←	What noises are you used to hearing in your neighborhood? ←
What time are you used to waking up? →	What time did you use to wake up as a child? →	What is something you used to do, but don't do now? →	What are you used to eating in the morning?
Finish! ←	How much traffic are you used to in your neighborhood? ←	What is something you didn't use to do, but do now? ←	What kind of food did you use to eat as a child?

B **Share** information about your classmates.

> Julia used to play in the park with her sister for fun.

> Oswaldo is used to going to the supermarket once a week.

3 Wrap up

Complete the **Self-assessment** on page 138.

☑ Scan ads to get key information about volunteer positions; contrast *used to* and *be used to*   UNIT 5   **69**

LESSON A
Listening

1 **Before you listen**

A What do you see?

B What is happening?

Unit
Goals

Express opinions about technology

Identify advantages and disadvantages of technology

Predict how technology may change lives in the future

STUDENT TK 22
CLASS CD2 TK 2

STUDENT TK 22
CLASS CD2 TK 2

2 Listen

A Listen and answer the questions.

1. Who are the speakers?   2. What are they talking about?

B Listen again. Complete the chart.

	Time-saving device	Opinion about time-saving device
1. Mrs. Rosen	*address stamper*	
2. Mr. Chung		
3. Ms. Morales		

3 After you listen

A Read. Complete the story.

convenient	distracting	innovative	spam
devices	electronic	manual	text message

Today, a reporter from KESL Radio asked three people about technology and

their favorite time-saving _____*devices*_____. Mrs. Rosen's favorite device is
            1

_____. She says it saves time, even though it isn't _____.
        2   3

Mr. Chung isn't a fan of technology. In fact, he says technology *wastes* more time

than it saves. For example, he says he doesn't like e-mail because he gets lots of

_____. He also finds e-mail _____. He doesn't think it is
        4   5

_____. Ms. Morales loves technology. She uses the camera on her cell
        6

phone in a very _____ way – to send her daughter pictures of clothes
                    7

that are on sale. Her daughter sends a _____ back: "Buy." or "Don't buy."
                                            8

STUDENT TK 23
CLASS CD2 TK 3

Listen and check your answers.

B Discuss. Talk with your classmates.

1. Do you agree with the people interviewed? Why or why not?

2. In general, do you think technology saves time or wastes time? Give examples.

☑ Listen for and identify people's opinions about technology   **UNIT 6**   **71**

LESSON **B** Clauses of concession

1 Grammar focus: *although*

> **Although** e-mail is fast, Mr. Chung doesn't like to use it.

> Mr. Chung doesn't like to use e-mail **although** it is fast.

Turn to page 145 for a grammar explanation.

2 Practice

A **Write.** Combine the sentences. Use *although*.

1. Mr. Green doesn't use a microwave. He buys lots of frozen food.
   Although Mr. Green doesn't use a microwave, he buys lots of frozen food.

2. Ms. White's car has a GPS system. She gets lost all the time.
   _____

3. Mr. Wang doesn't have a laptop computer. He travels constantly.
   _____

4. Mrs. Sanchez can't operate her digital camera. She read the instructions three times.
   _____

5. Mrs. Belcanto doesn't want a dishwasher. She has six children.
   _____

6. Ms. Kaye had urgent business in another state. She refused to travel by plane.
   _____

7. My house has central air-conditioning. I prefer to use a fan when it's hot.
   _____

8. My grandmother doesn't use e-mail. She has an e-mail address.
   _____

9. MP3 players are very popular. I still listen to music on a CD player.
   _____

CLASS CD2 TK 4

Listen and check your answers.

B Talk with a partner. Choose pairs of pictures and make sentences about Mr. Chung. Use *although* and *even though* with verbs from the box.

| clean | find information | have | listen | use | wash | write |

> Even though Mr. Chung has a computer, he prefers to write letters by hand.

USEFUL LANGUAGE

even though = although

1.

2.
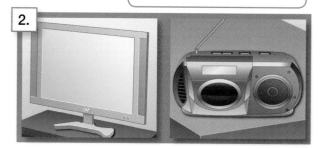

3.

4.

5.
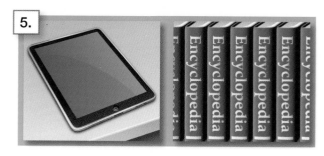

6.

Write sentences about Mr. Chung.

Although Mr. Chung has a computer, he prefers to write letters by hand.

3 Communicate

A Work in a small group. Talk about time-saving devices or tools that you own but don't use. Give reasons. Use *although* and *even though*.

A Although I have a food processor, I almost never use it.
B Why?
A It's too hard to clean.

CULTURE NOTE

In the United States, many people hold garage or yard sales to sell household items they no longer use.

B Share information about your classmates.

LESSON C Clauses of reason and concession

1 Grammar focus: contrasting *because* and *although*

> **Because** cable Internet is fast, many people want it.
>
> **Although** cable Internet is fast, many people cannot afford it.

Turn to page 145 for a grammar explanation.

2 Practice

A Write. Complete the story. Use *because* or *although*.

Pam

Beth

Although Pam and Beth are sisters, they are very different. Pam is very
₁

modern. She loves electrical appliances _____ they are fast and convenient.
₂

For example, she loves her microwave _____ she can use it to thaw meat
₃

quickly. She enjoys shopping for the latest kitchen devices, _____ some of
₄

them are very expensive. Beth has a different attitude about modern technology. She

prefers not to use electrical appliances. For instance, she never uses a microwave

_____ she thinks the radiation is bad. She dries her clothes outside on
₅

a line _____ she likes their smell after they've been in the fresh air. She
₆

washes her dishes by hand _____ she says dishwashers waste energy. Pam
₇

doesn't understand why Beth is so old-fashioned. But _____ the sisters have
₈

different lifestyles, they appreciate and enjoy one another very much.

Listen and check your answers.

B Talk with a partner. Compare Mr. Speedy and Mr. Thrifty. Use *because* and *although*.

> Although the subway is cheaper, Mr. Speedy drives to work.

> Mr. Thrifty takes the subway to work because it's cheaper.

Mr. Speedy	Mr. Thrifty
drives to work	takes the subway to work
shops online	shops in stores
buys his lunch	brings lunch from home
travels by plane	travels by train
looks up phone numbers on the Internet	uses the phone book
buys cakes at a bakery	bakes his own cakes

Write sentences about Mr. Speedy and Mr. Thrifty.

Although the subway is cheaper, Mr. Speedy drives to work.

Mr. Thrifty takes the subway to work because it's cheaper.

3 Communicate

A Work with a partner. Ask and answer questions about the activities in Exercise 2B. Give reasons for your answers.

> A Do you drive to work or take public transportation?
> B Well, although driving is faster, I take public transportation.
> A Why?
> B Because I don't have a car!

USEFUL LANGUAGE

Use *neither* when the answer to both choices in a question is negative.

A *Do you drive to work or take public transportation?*

B *Neither. I ride my bike.*

B Share information about your partner.

LESSON **D** Reading

1 Before you read

Talk with your classmates. Answer the questions.

1. How has technology changed transportation?
2. How has technology impacted the way we communicate with others?

2 Read

STUDENT TK 24
CLASS CD2 TK 6

Read the magazine article. Listen and read again.

The **Impact** of **Technology**

By Katelyn Houston

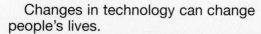

Changes in technology can change people's lives.

When my great-grandmother was born in 1900, her family lived on a ranch, and they went to town in a horse and buggy. Cars were rare; people thought they were dangerous pieces of machinery. By the time my great-grandmother died in 1979, nearly everyone owned a car, and horse buggies were in museums.

Although transportation technology has not changed significantly in my own lifetime, there have been huge changes in the way we get the news. Newspapers were once people's primary source for the news: in 1965, 72 percent of Americans reported that they read a newspaper on an average day. By 2005, that number was down to 50 percent. Today hardly anyone reads the newspaper! Another common way that people got news in the past was by listening to the radio, which began to broadcast news in the 1920s. I suppose nearly everyone had a radio then. However, by the 1950s, television was overtaking radio. Now even the number of people watching the news on television has declined, dropping from 60 percent in 1993 to 28 percent in 2006. So what's the latest source for news? The Web. The number of Americans who use the Internet to get the news is increasing. Most people access the news on their smart phones.

Yet another example of change is how we pay for goods and services. Until the mid-1940s, people had to carry large amounts of cash in their purses and wallets. Then, one day in 1949, when a man named Frank McNamara took some business associates to dinner, he left his wallet at home. He had to call his wife to bring him money to pay the bill. I think it was probably the most embarrassing moment of his life!

Mr. McNamara vowed to find a way to avoid carrying cash. Some stores already had their own charge cards, but there was no single, multi-purpose credit card. A year later he returned to the same restaurant with the same people, but paid with the credit card he had created, called "Diner's Club." A year after that second dinner, 42,000 people in the United States had the card, and two years after that, the card was also used in Canada, Cuba, Mexico, and the United Kingdom. I bet that paying with plastic will soon be as antiquated as the horse and buggy. Already, many people pay for things with their smartphones.

In what other ways do you think technology may change our lives in the future?

3 After you read

A Check your understanding.

Look at the reading tip. Then write *F* for fact or *O* for opinion, based on the reading.

> Critical readers recognize the difference between *facts* and *opinions*. Facts are known or proven. Opinions are feelings or beliefs.

___F__ 1. The author's great-grandmother was born in 1900.

_____ 2. By 2006, only 28 percent of Americans got their news by television.

_____ 3. Nearly everyone had a radio in the 1920s.

_____ 4. In 1965, 72 percent of Americans read a newspaper most days.

_____ 5. Frank McNamara was embarrassed because he didn't have cash to pay for dinner.

_____ 6. McNamara created the Diner's Club credit card.

_____ 7. The author thinks that paying with plastic will soon be antiquated.

_____ 8. In 1900, people thought cars were dangerous pieces of machinery.

B Build your vocabulary.

1. Read the dictionary entry. How many definitions are there?

> **rare** /*adj*/ **1** not common **2** slightly cooked – **rarely** /*adv*/; **rarity** /*n*/

2. Find the words in the story. Underline the sentence. Determine the part of speech. Use a dictionary to find the definition that fits the reading. Write related words and their part of speech.

Vocabulary	Definition	Related words and part of speech
1. rare *(adj)*	*not common*	*rarely (adverb)* *rarity (noun)*
2. primary		
3. source		
4. bet		
5. decline		
6. moment		

C Talk with a partner.

1. What is your primary source for getting the news?
2. What would you like to buy if prices declined?
3. Share a very embarrassing moment or a very happy moment in your life.

LESSON E Writing

1 Before you write

A **Work** in a small group. Make a list of time-saving devices you and your classmates use. Write one advantage and one disadvantage of each.

Device	Advantage	Disadvantage
calculator	does math quickly	breaks easily
1.		
2.		
3.		
4.		
5.		
6.		
7.		
8.		

B **Read** the paragraph.

My Favorite Time-saving Device

My favorite time-saving device, voice mail, has many advantages, but it also has some disadvantages. Before I had voice mail, I used to answer my phone every time it rang, even if I was busy. But with voice mail, I don't have to interrupt my work. The caller can just leave a message, and I can get it later. Another benefit of voice mail is that it allows me to avoid talking to people I don't want to talk to. But, of course, that is also a disadvantage because they can avoid talking to me! Another problem is that not only friends leave messages. Sometimes there are voice-mail messages from salespeople. So even though voice mail is very convenient, it has drawbacks as well.

> One way of organizing a paragraph is by describing advantages and disadvantages.

C **Work** with a partner. Complete the diagram of the model paragraph.

don't have to interrupt work

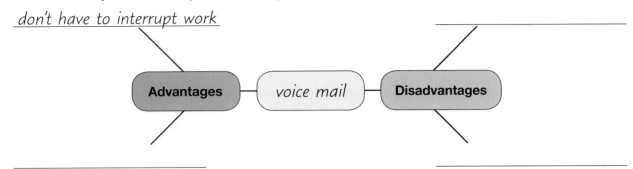

Advantages — voice mail — Disadvantages

D **Plan** a paragraph that discusses the advantages and disadvantages of a time-saving device. Use the diagram to make notes on your ideas.

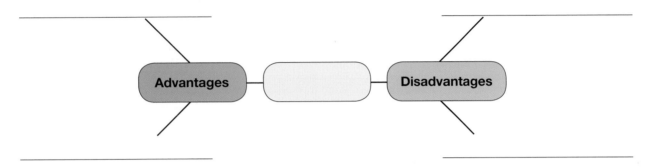

Advantages — Disadvantages

2 Write

Write a paragraph about a time-saving device. Give the paragraph a title, include a topic sentence, and describe at least two advantages and two disadvantages. Use the paragraph in Exercise 1B and the diagrams in Exercises 1C and 1D to help you.

3 After you write

A **Check** your writing.

	Yes	No
1. My paragraph has a title.	☐	☐
2. My topic sentence names the time-saving device.	☐	☐
3. I described at least two advantages and two disadvantages.	☐	☐

B **Share** your writing with a partner.

1. Take turns. Read your paragraph to a partner.
2. Comment on your partner's paragraph. Ask your partner a question about the paragraph. Tell your partner one thing you learned.

☑ Write a paragraph that discusses advantages and disadvantages   **UNIT 6**   **79**

LESSON F Another view

Internet Activities of Adults in Green County

Activity	2002	2007	2012
Bank online	3%	8%	18%
Get news online	12%	18%	30%
Join a social network	—	3%	15%
Play online games	5%	24%	36%
Send or read e-mail	25%	33%	45%
Shop online		2%	8%
Use a search engine	—	24%	38%
Watch a video online		5%	14%

A Read the questions. Look at the table. Fill in the answer.

1. In 2002, the most popular use of the Internet was _____.

   (A) sending and reading e-mail

   (B) banking online

   (C) using a search engine

   (D) none of the above

2. In 2007, fewer than 5 percent of the people in the survey used the Internet _____.

   (A) to shop online

   (B) to join a social network

   (C) to watch a video online

   (D) both *a* and *b*

3. From 2002 to 2007, the greatest increase in Internet use was _____.

   (A) playing online games

   (B) sending and receiving e-mail

   (C) using a search engine

   (D) none of the above

4. In 2012, banking online was more popular than _____.

   (A) joining a social network

   (B) watching a video online

   (C) shopping online

   (D) all of the above

5. From 2007 to 2012, the percentage increase in people who get news online was greater than the percentage increase in people who _____.

   (A) watch a video online

   (B) shop online

   (C) bank online

   (D) all of the above

6. In 2007, playing online games was not more popular than _____.

   (A) joining a social network

   (B) using a search engine

   (C) shopping online

   (D) banking online

B Talk with your classmates. Which activities in the table do you think will become more popular or less popular in the future? Why?

2 Grammar connections: *so* and *such*

so + adjective	*such* + adjective + noun
That clock is **so** <u>small</u> (that it's hard to see the time).	That's **such** <u>a small clock</u> (that it's hard to see the time).
Those cars are **so** <u>nice</u> (that I want to drive them).	Those are **such** <u>nice cars</u> (that I want to drive them).

A Talk with a partner. Describe the pictures with *so* and *such*. Take turns.

> A That watch is so old (that no one would use it).
> B That is such an old watch (that no one would use it).

B Work in a small group. Describe items in the word box with your own information. Use *so* and *such*. Take turns.

> your Internet connection at home   your commute to work / school
> your house / apartment / room   your cell phone
> your television   your watch

> A I have such a fast Internet connection at home that I can watch videos online easily.
> B You're lucky! My Internet connection at home is so slow that I don't use it very often.

3 Wrap up

Complete the **Self-assessment** on page 138.

Review

1 Listening

CLASS CD2 TK 7

Listen. Take notes on a radio interview.

Characteristics of tutors	Requirements to be a tutor
1. *compassionate — care about helping*	4.
2.	5.
3.	6.

Talk with a partner. Check your answers.

2 Grammar

A Write. Complete the story.

A Love of Technology

My friend Bob loves technology. ___*As soon as*___ a new computer

              1. As soon as / Until

comes out, he buys it. The same is true with his cell phone. He doesn't wait

_____ the end of his contract. _____ his
  2. as soon as / until   3. Because / Even though

cell phone is still good, he buys a new one. _____ he loves the
                            4. Because / Even though

latest technology, his house is filled with new devices. _____
                                   5. Although / Until

he has the newest devices, he keeps the old ones. His wife is unhappy. She has

told him, "No more electronic gadgets _____ you get rid of the
                    6. as soon as / until

old ones."

B Write. Look at the words that are underlined in the answers. Write the questions.

1. A _____

   B <u>Bob</u> loves technology.

2. A _____

   B He buys a new cell phone <u>as soon as</u>
      <u>a new one comes out</u>.

3. A _____

   B His house is filled with <u>new devices</u>.

4. A _____

   B <u>Because of all the electronic gadgets</u>,
      Bob's wife is unhappy.

Talk with a partner. Ask and answer the questions.

3 Pronunciation: stressed and unstressed words

Content words (nouns, main verbs, adverbs, adjectives, negatives, and question words) are usually stressed. Function words (pronouns, prepositions, conjunctions, articles, *be* verbs, and auxiliary verbs) are usually not stressed.

CLASS CD2 TK 8

A **Listen** to the stressed and unstressed words in each sentence. The stressed words are underlined.

1. <u>Pam</u> <u>loves</u> <u>electrical</u> <u>appliances</u> because they <u>save</u> her <u>time</u>.
2. She <u>wants</u> to <u>volunteer</u> in the <u>health-care field</u>.
3. Even though <u>computers</u> are <u>time-savers</u>, <u>some</u> <u>people</u> <u>don't</u> <u>use</u> them.
4. Will he <u>go</u> to <u>sleep</u> as soon as his <u>visitors</u> <u>leave</u>?

Listen again and repeat. Stress the underlined content words.

CLASS CD2 TK 9

B **Listen and repeat.** Then underline the stressed content words.

1. She delivers meals to seniors.
2. Volunteers should be patient and compassionate.
3. Do you walk to work or drive?
4. Mr. Chung isn't a fan of e-mail.

Read your sentences to a partner. Compare your answers.

C **Read** the paragraph. Underline the stressed words.

> Ingrid worked with computers in her native country, so she wants a job working with computers in the U.S. She's been looking for several months, but she hasn't found a job yet. Finally, she decided to do some volunteer work until she could find a paying job. Ingrid volunteers at the local zoo. She does office work on the computer.

Talk with a partner. Compare your answers. Read the paragraph to your partner.

D **Write** four sentences from Units 5 and 6. Then work with a partner. Underline the stressed words in your partner's sentences.

1. _____
2. _____
3. _____
4. _____

LESSON **A**
Listening

1 **Before you listen**

A What do you see?

B What is happening?

1.

2.

Unit Goals

Identify store policies for returning items

Identify pros and cons of online shopping

Interpret a returned-merchandise form

2 Listen

STUDENT TK 25
CLASS CD2 TK 10

A **Listen** and answer the questions.

1. Who are the speakers?   2. What are they talking about?

STUDENT TK 25
CLASS CD2 TK 10

B **Listen again.** Complete the chart.

1. kind of camera Rosa bought	*a digital camera*
2. problem	
3. date purchased	
4. today's date	
5. store policy for refunds	
6. store policy for exchanges	

3 After you listen

A **Read.** Complete the story.

condition	defective	merchandise	store credit
customer service	exchanges	refund	warranty

> Rosa wants to return the camera that she bought and get a ___refund___ . She
>
> is told that she needs to speak with someone in _____. The clerk there asks
>   2
>
> Rosa if the camera is _____, and she says it isn't. The clerk tells her about the
>   3
>
> store policy for returns and _____. It's too late for Rosa to return the camera,
>   4
>
> but she can exchange it if the _____ is in perfect _____. Rosa still has
>   5   6
>
> the camera box with the instruction book and the _____ card. Since Rosa is in
>   7
>
> a hurry, she decides to get a _____, and she will use it at a later time.
>   8

STUDENT TK 26
CLASS CD2 TK 11

Listen and check your answers.

B **Discuss.** Talk with your classmates.

1. What are some reasons that people may want to return merchandise to a store?
2. What are some situations where it may be impossible to return merchandise?
3. Do you think people should get a refund for something they have used? Why or why not?

LESSON **B** Subject-pattern adjective clauses

1 Grammar focus: *that* and *who*

Simple sentences	Sentences with an adjective clause
The **camera** costs only $99. It is on sale.	The **camera that is on sale** costs only $99.
The manager helped the **customer**. She lost her receipt.	The manager helped the **customer who lost her receipt**.

Turn to page 145 for a grammar explanation.

2 Practice

A Write. Combine the sentences. Change the second sentence into an adjective clause with *that* or *who*.

1. I want to buy a camera. It's not too expensive.

   I want to buy a camera that's not too expensive.

2. I'd like to get a good camera. It will last for many years.

   _____

3. Many people shop online. They are looking for cameras.

   _____

4. My friend told me about a camera store. It sells used merchandise.

   _____

5. Customers like to shop at Super Camera. They appreciate good service.

   _____

6. The clerk is very helpful. He works in customer service.

   _____

7. These days, many people want an expensive camera. It has separate lenses.

   _____

8. Smart phones are convenient to use. They have cameras.

   _____

> **USEFUL** LANGUAGE
>
> - Adjective clauses that describe people begin with *that* or *who*.
> - Adjective clauses that describe things begin with *that* or *which*.

Listen and check your answers.

CLASS CD2 TK 12

B **Talk** with a partner. Ask and answer questions to identify the following people in the picture: the cashier, the cleaning person, the customer, the greeter, the stock clerk, and the store manager. Use adjective clauses with *that*, *who*, or *which*. Choose verbs from the box.

clean	have	listen	smile	sweep
give	hold	put	stand	wear

> **A** Which one is the cashier?
> **B** He's the man who's putting the video camera into the bag.

> **A** You mean the one who's standing behind the counter?
> **B** Right.

Write sentences about the people in the picture.

The cashier is the man who's putting the video camera into the bag.

3 Communicate

A **Work** in a small group. Ask and answer questions about the topics. Use adjective clauses with *that*, *who*, or *which*.

> **A** Nadia, what kinds of supermarkets do you like?
> **B** I like supermarkets that are open 24 hours a day. What about you, Phuong?
> **C** I like supermarkets that have lots of fresh fish.

- clothing stores
- malls
- restaurants
- salesclerks
- supermarkets
- (your idea)

B **Share** information about your classmates.

LESSON C Object-pattern adjective clauses

1 Grammar focus: *that*

Simple sentences	Sentences with an adjective clause
I like the **car**. You bought it.	I like the **car (that) you bought**.
The **mechanic** has 20 years of experience. I use him.	The **mechanic (that) I use** has 20 years of experience.

Turn to page 145 for a grammar explanation.

Turn to page 145 for a grammar explanation.

USEFUL LANGUAGE

The word *that* is optional when it is the object of the dependent clause.

2 Practice

A Write. Combine the sentences. Change the second sentence into an adjective clause with *that*.

1. Suzy is a good friend. I've known her for several years.

   Suzy is a good friend that I've known for several years.

2. Last January, her old car stopped working. She was driving it.

   _____

3. The mechanic couldn't fix it. Her friend recommended the mechanic.

   _____

4. Finally, she decided to buy a used car from a man. She knew the man at work.

   _____

5. He's an honest person. She trusts him completely.

   _____

6. He gave her a good price. She couldn't refuse it.

   _____

7. The used car is only three years old. He sold her the car.

   _____

8. It's a reliable car. She can drive it for a long time.

   _____

Listen and check your answers.

CLASS CD2 TK 13

B **Talk** with a partner. Ted and Lisa got married recently. Unfortunately, they have had some bad luck. Look at the chart and make sentences by choosing an item from each column.

> The dishes that Ted and Lisa received from Aunt May were broken.

dishes	found on the Internet	the wrong size
computer	bought on sale	scratched
car	ordered from a catalog	broken
camera	got as a wedding present	damaged
rug	received from Aunt May	torn
lamps	picked up at a garage sale	the wrong color
coffee table	purchased from a friend	too slow

Write sentences about Ted and Lisa.

The dishes they received from Aunt May were broken.

3 Communicate

A **Work** in a small group. Tell about a shopping "mistake." Include the information below.

- What was the item?
- When did you buy it?
- Where did you buy it?
- What was wrong with it?
- What did you do about it?

> **A** The chicken that I bought last week at Paglia's Meats was spoiled.
> **B** What did you do about it?
> **A** I took it back to the store and asked them to give me a fresh package.

USEFUL LANGUAGE

Use the following adjectives to say what is wrong with something you bought: *broken, defective, damaged, spoiled, torn, too big, too small.*

B **Share** information about your classmates.

LESSON **D** Reading

1 Before you read

Talk with your classmates. Answer the questions.

1. Have you ever tried to exchange an item or get a refund? Describe your experience.
2. In your native country, is it easy or difficult for people to get a refund for something that they purchased?

2 Read

STUDENT TK 27
CLASS CD2 TK 14

Read the newspaper advice column. Listen and read again.

> Sometimes an important word is replaced by a synonym. This makes the reading more interesting. For example, *seller* and *retailer* are two nouns that have the same meaning.

The Smart Shopper

Dear Smart Shopper,

I'm a jewelry lover, and I enjoy shopping online. Unfortunately, I just bought a pair of gold earrings that I don't like. When I tried to return them, I learned that the seller has a no-return policy. Don't I have the right to get a refund?

Mad Madelyn

Dear Mad Madelyn,

If the merchandise is defective, the seller must return your money or make an exchange. However, if the merchandise was in good condition when you received it, and if the retailer has a no-return policy, there is nothing you can do. This is true for store purchases as well as Internet purchases. In the future, here are some questions you should ask before you buy anything:

- Does the seller say "satisfaction guaranteed or your money back"?

- Is there a time limit on returns, such as two weeks?

- Who pays the shipping costs on items that are returned?

- Do you need to return the merchandise in its original package?

- Is the original receipt required?

- Does the retailer give a store credit instead of a cash refund?

- If the retailer has a store in your area, can you return the merchandise to the store instead of shipping it?

Next time, find the return policy on the merchant's Web site and print it, or ask the merchant for the return policy in writing. It's important to get all the facts that you need before you buy!

Smart Shopper

3 After you read

A Check your understanding.

1. What is Madelyn's problem?
2. If an item is defective, does a purchaser have the right to return it?
3. Does Madelyn have the right to get a refund? Why or why not?
4. Is the Smart Shopper's advice for Internet purchases, store purchases, or both?
5. What should Madelyn have done before she bought the earrings?
6. What is the meaning of "satisfaction guaranteed or your money back"?
7. *Seller* and *retailer* are synonyms. What is another word in the reading with the same meaning?
8. Smart Shopper lists several questions that purchasers should ask before they buy. In your opinion, which question is the most important? Why?

B Build your vocabulary.

Compound nouns are noun + noun combinations that have special meanings. Sometimes you can explain compound nouns with adjective clauses. For example, a *jewelry lover* is a person who loves jewelry.

1. Find compound nouns in the reading that match the meanings. Write them on the chart.

Compound noun	Meaning
1. *jewelry lover*	a person who loves jewelry
2.	a limit that is related to time
3.	costs that are related to shipping
4.	a credit that is given by a store
5.	a refund that is made in cash
6.	a policy that is related to returns
7.	
8.	

2. Find two more compound nouns in the reading. Write them on the chart. Use adjective clauses to explain what they mean.
3. Work in a small group. Make a list of other compound nouns you know. Use adjective clauses to explain what they mean.

C Talk with a partner.

1. Are you a jewelry lover? What do you love to buy?
2. What's the most you have paid in shipping costs? What was it for?
3. Have you ever gotten a cash refund? For what? Why?

☑ Recognize synonyms in a reading and reasons for using them;
identify and explain the meanings of compound nouns **UNIT 7** **91**

LESSON E Writing

1 Before you write

A Talk with a partner. List some reasons people should or shouldn't shop online.

Reasons people should shop online	Reasons people shouldn't shop online
It's convenient.	*It's hard to choose merchandise you can't touch.*

B Read the paragraph.

Reasons You Shouldn't Shop Online

There are some good reasons you shouldn't shop online. First, it's hard to choose merchandise that you can't touch. For example, a piece of jewelry might look very good on the computer screen, but after you buy it and look at it closely, you may find that it's very ugly and poorly made. Furthermore, shopping online is slow. It may take several days to receive the merchandise. If you are not satisfied, it may take weeks to exchange the merchandise or get your money back. Finally, shopping online can be dangerous. People can steal your credit card number and use it to buy expensive items. An irresponsible seller can take your money and never send you the merchandise. I'm going to do my shopping in stores!

> Use transition words such as *first, second, next, furthermore, moreover,* and *finally* to signal a list of reasons in a paragraph.

C **Complete** the outline with information from the model paragraph.

Transition words   **Reasons and supporting details**

First   First reason: *hard to choose merchandise you can't touch*

                                         Supporting detail: _____

_____   Second reason: _____

                                         Supporting detail: _____

                                         Supporting detail: _____

_____   Third reason: _____

                                         Supporting detail: _____

                                         Supporting detail: _____

D **Plan** a paragraph about why you *should* shop online. Think of two or more reasons and one or more supporting details for each reason. Make notes about your ideas in an outline like the one in Exercise 1C. Use your own paper.

2 Write

Write a paragraph about why you should shop online. Give at least two reasons and one supporting detail for each reason. Use transition words to signal your list of reasons. Use the paragraph in Exercise 1B and the outlines in Exercises 1C and 1D to help you.

3 After you write

A **Check** your writing.

	Yes	No
1. I wrote two or more reasons to shop online.	☐	☐
2. I gave one or more supporting details for each reason.	☐	☐
3. I used transition words like *first*, *furthermore*, and *finally* to signal my list of reasons.	☐	☐

B **Share** your writing with a partner.

1. Take turns. Read your paragraph to a partner.
2. Comment on your partner's paragraph. Ask your partner a question about the paragraph. Tell your partner one thing you learned.

☑ Write a paragraph that provides reasons and examples to support an opinion; use transition words to signal a list of reasons

LESSON F Another view

Life-skills reading

JedsSports.com 🏒🏈

RETURNED-MERCHANDISE FORM

Please complete this form and send it with the returned merchandise within 21 days to JedsSports.com, 3209 W. Foster Ave., Chicago, IL 60625. Include a copy of the invoice and the original packaging. Call us for a Returned-Merchandise Authorization number (M–F, 8 a.m.–5 p.m., CST) at 800-555-4143.

Name: *Rita Miller*   **RMA#:** *98704370*

Check one:
☐ Store Credit
☑ Exchange

Address *271 Dade Drive* **City** *Largo* **State** *FL* **Zip** *33771*

List items for return:

Item #	Description	Size	Color	Reason	Additional Comments
P4103	*sweatshirt*	*medium*	*red*	*wrong size*	*I ordered a large.*

List items to receive in exchange:

Item #	Description	Size	Color		
P4128	*sweatshirt*	*large*	*red*		

A Read the questions. Look at the returned-merchandise form. Fill in the answer.

1. Why is the buyer using this form?
   - Ⓐ She wants her money back.
   - Ⓑ She wants a store credit.
   - Ⓒ She wants to exchange the merchandise.
   - Ⓓ none of the above

2. What does the buyer need to include with this form?
   - Ⓐ the invoice
   - Ⓑ the item that she is returning
   - Ⓒ the original packaging
   - Ⓓ all of the above

3. Which statement is true?
   - Ⓐ The buyer must return the items within 21 days.
   - Ⓑ The buyer is satisfied with her purchase.
   - Ⓒ The buyer needs a smaller sweatshirt.
   - Ⓓ The buyer lives in New Jersey.

4. Which statement is not true?
   - Ⓐ The buyer is returning one item.
   - Ⓑ The buyer needs a different size.
   - Ⓒ The merchandise was defective.
   - Ⓓ The buyer wants the same color.

5. What does "RMA#" mean?
   - Ⓐ returned-merchandise invoice number
   - Ⓑ returned-merchandise authorization number
   - Ⓒ credit card number
   - Ⓓ none of the above

6. How did Rita get the RMA number?
   - Ⓐ She e-mailed the store.
   - Ⓑ She called an 800 number.
   - Ⓒ She got it from the original invoice.
   - Ⓓ It was written on the merchandise.

B Talk with your classmates. Do you think it is difficult to return or exchange merchandise at this store? Why or why not?

2 **Grammar connections:** Clarifying questions

Statement	Clarifying questions
I went <u>to the mall</u>.	You went **where**?
There was a sale <u>last weekend</u>.	There was a sale **when**?
I bought some <u>shirts</u>.	You bought some **what**?
They were <u>$20</u> each.	They were **how much**?
I bought <u>five</u> of them.	You bought **how many**?
They're for <u>my sister</u>.	They're for **who**?

A Complete the paragraph to make a story. Then talk with a partner.
Your partner will listen and ask a clarifying question after every sentence.
Answer your partner's question.

> A I needed to buy a laptop case.
> B You needed to buy what?
> A A laptop case.

I needed to buy _____. So I went to _____. I
                       1   2
got there at _____ o'clock. I couldn't find any, so I talked to
                  3
_____. That person told me to go _____. Finally I
    4   5
found one. It only cost $ _____. I didn't buy just one. I bought
                              6
_____! I took them home and showed them to _____.
    7   8
He / She / They said, "_____!"
                   9

B Share your partner's story with the class. The class will ask clarifying questions.

> A Luis needed to buy a laptop case.
> Class He needed to buy what?
> A A laptop case.

3 **Wrap up**

Complete the **Self-assessment** on page 139.

LESSON A
Listening

1 Before you listen

A What do you see?

B What is happening?

Unit Goals
Identify problems at work and school
Provide solutions and identify consequences to those solutions
Describe hard and soft skills

UNIT 8

2 Listen

STUDENT TK 28
CLASS CD2 TK 15

A Listen and answer the questions.

1. Who are the speakers?   2. What are they talking about?

STUDENT TK 28
CLASS CD2 TK 15

B Listen again. Complete the diagram.

```
                  _____
                       Yolanda's problem
                              |
1. _____  —  ( Possible solutions )  —  4. _____

          2. _____        3. _____

                  _____
                       Yolanda's decision
```

3 After you listen

A Read. Complete the story.

chart	deal with	initials	share
close up	exhausted	negotiate	work (something) out

Yolanda and David work at Daria's Donut Shop. Lately, David has been leaving

work early, and Yolanda has to ___*close up*___ the shop by herself. Tonight, Yolanda is
                                    1

having coffee with her friends. She is _____. Her friends give her advice. Teresa
                                            2

thinks she should talk to her boss, but Yolanda wants to try to _____ things
                                                                        3

_____ with David first. Julie thinks Yolanda should make a _____
      3   4

of their duties. Then she should _____ with David and decide who is going to
                                        5

do which tasks. When they finish a task, they should write their _____ on the
                                                                        6

chart. If David isn't doing his _____ of the work, it will show in the chart. Then,
                                    7

Yolanda can show the chart to their boss and let her _____ the situation.
                                                            8

STUDENT TK 29
CLASS CD2 TK 16

Listen and check your answers.

B Discuss. Talk with your classmates.

Have you ever had a problem at work or school? How did you solve it?

LESSON B Verb tense contrast

1 Grammar focus: present perfect and present perfect continuous

Present perfect (recently finished action)	Present perfect continuous (continuing action)
Yolanda **has (just) mopped** the floor. It's clean now.	Yolanda **has been mopping** the floor **for** 15 minutes.

Turn to page 146 for complete grammar charts and explanations.
Turn to page 149 for a list of past participles.

2 Practice

A Write. Complete the sentences. Use the present perfect or present perfect continuous forms of the verbs. Use *just* where possible.

1. Daria Thompson is the owner of Daria's Donut Shop.

   She ____has been selling____ donuts at this location
   (sell)
   for more than 20 years.

2. It's 7:00 a.m. Daria _____ donuts
   (make)
   for three hours.

3. It's 7:30 a.m. Daria _____ the shop
   (open)
   for customers.

4. It's 10:30 a.m. Daria's son _____
   (help)
   her all morning.

5. He _____ cleaning the counters and shelves. Everything is spotless.
   (finish)

6. Daria needs more help in the shop. She _____ to hire Yolanda.
   (decide)

7. Yolanda's shift begins at 6:00 a.m. today. She _____ for the bus for
   (wait)
   30 minutes. She's worried that she's going to be late.

8. It's 6:05 a.m. Yolanda _____ to say she will be late.
   (call)

 Listen and check your answers.

CLASS CD2 TK 17

98 UNIT 8

B **Talk** with a partner. Look at Yolanda's work schedule. Make sentences about the things she has just done and has been doing at the following times: 6:15, 6:30, 7:30, 11:00, 12:00, 2:00, and 4:00.

> It's 6:15 a.m. Yolanda has just arrived.

> It's 11:00 a.m. Yolanda has been serving customers for three and a half hours.

Yolanda's Schedule

6:15 a.m.	Arrive Turn off the security alarm
6:30 a.m.	Open the cash register Make coffee
7:30 a.m.	Open the shop for customers
7:30 a.m.–11:00 a.m.	Serve customers Take phone orders
11:00 a.m.–12:00 noon	Eat lunch Go to the bank
12:00 noon–4:00 p.m.	Serve customers Take phone orders
2:00 p.m.	Refill sugar containers Receive shipment of coffee
4:00 p.m.	Go home

Write sentences about Yolanda's schedule.

It's 6:15 a.m. Yolanda has just arrived.

It's 11:00 a.m. Yolanda has been serving customers for three and a half hours.

3 Communicate

A **Work** with a partner. Think about your own schedule. Your partner says a time. You say what you have been doing and what you have just done.

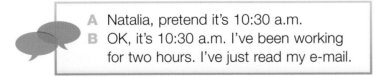

> A Natalia, pretend it's 10:30 a.m.
> B OK, it's 10:30 a.m. I've been working for two hours. I've just read my e-mail.

B **Share** information about your partner.

> It's 10:30 a.m. Natalia has been working for two hours. She has just read her e-mail.

LESSON C Participial adjectives

1 Grammar focus: adjectives ending in *-ed* and *-ing*

-ed adjectives	*-ing* adjectives	
I'm **tired** of this job.	This is a **tiring** job.	This job is **tiring**.
He's **interested** in this task.	This is an **interesting** task.	This task is **interesting**.
They're **disappointed** about their grades.	These are **disappointing** grades.	These grades are **disappointing**.

Turn to page 146 for a grammar explanation.

2 Practice

A Write. Circle the correct adjective.

1. A I heard that Juan and his friends went to a party after work. How was the party?

    B It was really (exciting)/ excited.

2. A How did Juan feel the next day at work?

    B He was **exhausting / exhausted**.

3. A How long did he have to work?

    B He had to work from 9:30 to 6:30. It was a **tiring / tired** day.

4. A Does Juan usually start working at 9:30?

    B No, he overslept! He was **shocking / shocked** that he didn't hear the alarm clock.

5. A How did his boss react when he showed up late?

    B His boss was **irritating / irritated**.

6. A What did his boss say to him?

    B He told Juan that he was **disappointing / disappointed** in him.

7. A Juan didn't have a good day, I guess. What did he do later that night?

    B He stayed home and had a **relaxing / relaxed** night in front of the TV.

8. A So, is Juan going to go out again on a weeknight?

    B I don't think so. He said it was an **exhausting / exhausted** experience.

CLASS CD2 TK 18

Listen and check your answers. Then practice with a partner.

B **Talk** with a partner. For each picture, describe the person and the activity. Choose participial adjectives from the boxes.

> The man is excited.

> Getting an award is exciting.

Positive		Negative	
amusing	amused	boring	bored
exciting	excited	frightening	frightened
interesting	interested	frustrating	frustrated

Write two sentences about each picture.

The man is excited.

Getting an award is exciting.

3 Communicate

A **Work** in a small group. Ask and answer questions about your experiences. Use the adjectives from Exercise 2B.

> A What's an amusing experience that you have had at work?
> B I was very amused when . . . It was amusing because . . .

B **Share** information about your classmates.

LESSON **D** Reading

1 Before you read

Talk with your classmates. Answer the questions.

1. What are some skills, such as following directions, that are necessary for most jobs?
2. What special skills do you have?

2 Read

Read the magazine article. Listen and read again.

STUDENT TK 30
CLASS CD2 TK 19

Hard and Soft Job Skills

Som Sarawong has been working as an automotive technician at George's Auto Repair for over five years. Today was a special day for Som, a 35-year-old Thai immigrant, because he received the Employee of the Year award. According to Ed Overton, Som's boss, Som received the award "because he's a great 'people person' and he has superb technical skills. I even have him work on my own car!"

Som has the two kinds of skills that are necessary to be successful and move up in his career: soft skills and hard skills. Soft skills are personal and social skills. Som gets along with his co-workers. He has a strong work ethic; in five years, he has never been late or absent from work. Customers trust him. Hard skills, on the other hand, are the technical skills a person needs to do a job. Som can repair cars,

trucks, and motorcycles. He learned from his father, who was also a mechanic. Then he took classes and got a certificate as an auto technician.

Soft and hard skills are equally important, but hard skills are easier to teach and assess than soft skills. People can learn how to use a machine and then take a test on their knowledge. However, it's harder to teach people how to be cooperative and have a good work ethic. George Griffith, the owner of George's Auto Repair, explains, "I've been working in this business for over 30 years, and most of the time when I've needed to fire someone, it was because of weak people skills, not because they didn't have technical abilities." Soft skills and good technical knowledge are a winning combination, and today, Som Sarawong was the winner.

3 After you read

A Check your understanding.

1. According to Som Sarawong's boss, why did Som get the Employee of the Year award?
2. What's the difference between a soft skill and a hard skill? Give examples.
3. Find two quotations in the reading. Underline them. What is the purpose of each quotation?
4. Which example shows that Som has a good work ethic?
5. Why is it easier to teach hard skills than soft skills?
6. According to what George Griffith says, do more workers lose their jobs because of weak soft skills or weak hard skills?
7. Do you agree with George Griffith? Why or why not?

> Quotations are used to explain or support a main idea. They also make a reading more interesting.

CULTURE NOTE

The expression *work ethic* is the belief that if you work hard in life you will get ahead and become successful.

B Build your vocabulary.

1. Find an example in the reading of each prefix and root. Write it in the chart.
2. Use a dictionary. Write the meaning of the words.
3. Guess the meaning of the prefixes and roots in the chart.

Prefixes	Example from reading	Meaning of word	Meaning of prefix
1. re-	*repair*	*to fix what is torn or broken*	*again*
2. co-			
3. auto-			
Roots			**Meaning of root**
4. tech			
5. super			
6. equ			

4. Work in a small group. Make a list of other words you know with the same prefixes and roots. Write a sentence for each new word.

C Talk with a partner.

1. What is something that you can do superbly?
2. What are some examples of technical skills?
3. What is a hobby or profession that requires good technical skills?
4. Are you good at repairing things? What can you repair?

LESSON **E** Writing

1 Before you write

A Talk with a partner. Answer the questions.

1. What is a cover letter? What information does it include?
2. Have you ever written a cover letter? Tell your partner about your experience.
3. Today, most people write e-mail cover letters. Why do you think this is true?

B Read the cover letter.

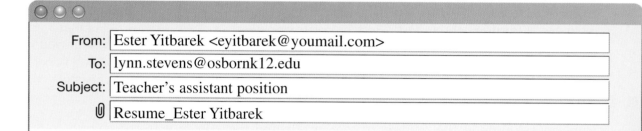

From: Ester Yitbarek <eyitbarek@youmail.com>
To: lynn.stevens@osbornk12.edu
Subject: Teacher's assistant position
🖇 Resume_Ester Yitbarek

Dear Ms. Stevens:

I read your advertisement online for a position as a teacher's assistant. I am very interested in this position and have attached my résumé.

I have been working as a teacher's assistant at Hilltop Elementary School for three years. In this job, I have taught reading and math to students in small groups. I have also tutored individual students who were having problems with the lessons. I'm very interested in child development, and I love working with children. I get along very well with my co-workers, and I'm also skilled at dealing with parents.

I am planning to move to a new home in your district. I hope you will call me to schedule an interview. My phone number is 773-555-2673. I look forward to hearing from you.

Sincerely,

Ester Yitbarek

> **CULTURE** NOTE
>
> Applicants are usually expected to include a résumé — a written statement of their educational and work experience — with their cover letter.

C Work with a partner. Answer the questions.

1. Who wrote the cover letter?
2. Who did she write it to?
3. What position is she applying for?
4. Where did she hear about the job?
5. How much experience does she have?
6. What are some of her skills?

> In the body of a cover letter, include:
> • the title of the job you are applying for
> • how you found out about the job
> • information about your skills and experience

D Plan a cover letter for a real or an imaginary job. Complete the information.

Paragraph 1:

1. Title of the job you are applying for: _____

2. How you found out about it: _____

Paragraph 2:

3. Your skills and experience: _____

_____

_____

2 Write

Write a cover letter for a real or an imaginary job that you are interested in. Include the title of the job in the first sentence and say how you found out about it. Give at least two examples of your skills and experience. Use the cover letter in Exercise 1B and your outline in Exercise 1D to help you.

3 After you write

A Check your writing.

	Yes	No
1. My first sentence says the title of the job I am applying for.	☐	☐
2. I included how I found out about the job.	☐	☐
3. I gave two or more examples of my skills and experience.	☐	☐

B Share your writing with a partner.

1. Take turns. Read your letter to a partner.
2. Comment on your partner's letter. Ask your partner a question about the letter. Tell your partner one thing you learned.

LESSON **F** Another view

1 Life-skills reading

The 30 fastest-growing occupations, 2010–2020 (in thousands)

Occupation	Employment		Change		Most significant source of postsecondary education or training
	2010	2020	Number	Percent	
Home health aides	1,018	1,724	706	69	Short-term on-the-job training
Biomedical engineers	16	26	10	63	Bachelor degree
Carpenters	46	72	26	56	Short-term on-the-job training
Physical therapist aides	47	67	20	43	none
Dental hygienists	182	250	68	37	Associate degree
Health educators	64	87	23	36	Bachelor degree

Source: http://data.bls.gov/cgi-bin/print.pl/news.release/ecopro.t07.htm

A **Read** the questions. Look at the chart. Fill in the answer.

1. Which occupation will grow the most from 2010 to 2020?
   - (A) biomedical engineers
   - (B) dental hygienists
   - (C) home health aides
   - (D) health educators

2. How many physical therapist aides will there be in 2020?
   - (A) 47
   - (B) 4,700
   - (C) 67
   - (D) 67,000

3. What percent of job growth will there be for carpenters from 2010 to 2020?
   - (A) 26
   - (B) 26,000
   - (C) 56
   - (D) 56,000

4. What is not true about dental hygienists?
   - (A) In 2020, there will be 68,000 more dental hygienists than in 2010.
   - (B) In 2010, there were 250,000 dental hygienists.
   - (C) It requires an associate degree.
   - (D) From 2010 to 2020, this job will grow by 37%.

B **Talk** with your classmates. Which job in the chart would you most like to have? What training do you need for it?

2 Grammar connections: polite requests and offers

	Questions	Answers	
Polite requests	**Would / Will you move** your chair? **Could / Can you help** me with this box? **Would you mind helping** me?	Sure. No problem. I'd be glad to.	I'd = I would that'd = that would
Offers	**Why don't I move** this box for you? **May / Can / Could I help** you with that? **Let me open** that for you.	OK, thanks. I'd appreciate it. That'd be great.	

A **Talk** with a partner. Use the pictures to make and respond to requests for the situation. Then use the pictures to make and respond to offers for the situation. Take turns.

> A Could you help me with this box?
> B Sure.

> B Let me move those books out of your way.
> A Thanks! That'd be great!

B **Talk** with a partner. Look at the places in the box. Have a conversation in each place. Make a request or offer in each conversation. Take turns.

a dark movie theater	an airplane	an office
a grocery store	a bus	a post office

> A It's dark in here. Would you mind helping me find my seat?
> B I'd be glad to. Follow me.
> A OK, thanks.

3 Wrap up

Complete the **Self-assessment** on page 139.

Review

1 Listening

Listen. Take notes on a class lecture.

CLASS CD2 TK 20

Job skills for an electronics store	Job skills for a restaurant
1. *good communication skills*	4.
2.	5.
3.	6.

Talk with a partner. Check your answers.

2 Grammar

A Write. Complete the story.

Joanie's Problem

Joanie is at the electronics store. She _____*has been talking*_____ with a clerk in
1. has talked / has been talking

customer service for the past 15 minutes. She wants to return a scanner. He told her she

could exchange the scanner. However, Joanie _____ at scanners
2. has looked / has been looking

for several months, and she still _____ another one she likes.
3. hasn't found / hasn't been finding

She wants a refund. The clerk _____ his manager this minute to
4. has just called / has been calling

see if Joanie can get a refund, but the manager is not in his office. This situation is very

_____ for Joanie. She's _____ and wants
5. frustrating / frustrated   6. tiring / tired

to go home.

B Write. Look at the words that are underlined in the answers. Write the questions.

1. A _____

   B Joanie wants to return her scanner.

2. A _____

   B Joanie has been talking to the clerk
   for 15 minutes.

3. A _____

   B The customer-service clerk says that
   she can exchange the scanner.

4. A _____

   B Joanie went to the store on Saturday
   afternoon.

Talk with a partner. Ask and answer the questions.

3 Pronunciation: stressing function words

Normally, function words such as pronouns, prepositions, conjunctions, articles, *to be* verbs, and auxiliary verbs are not stressed. However, when strong feelings or disagreements are expressed, function words can receive strong stress.

CLASS CD2 TK 21

A **Listen** to the stressed function words in each conversation.

1. A Is the camera defective?
   B It's defective <u>and</u> too small!

2. A Don't you usually finish at 5:00?
   B I <u>do</u> usually finish at 5:00, but not today.

3. A Why aren't you applying for that job?
   B I <u>am</u>. I'll go there tomorrow.

4. A I don't trust the man who sold you this car.
   B Well, <u>I do</u>! It's <u>my</u> decision, not <u>yours</u>.

5. A Is he excited about his new job?
   B No, but his wife <u>is</u>.

6. A Did you put the returned merchandise on my desk?
   B No, I put it <u>in</u> your desk.

Listen again and repeat. Stress the underlined function words.

CLASS CD2 TK 22

B **Listen and repeat.** Then underline the stressed function words.

1. A I'd like to exchange this sweater.
   B Why?
   A It's too big, and it has a hole.

2. A You can't leave early again!
   B Yes, I can and I will.

3. A Why don't you clean the counters?
   B Why don't you?

4. A Let's talk about a raise after you've worked here for six months.
   B Can we talk before six months?

Talk with a partner. Compare your answers.

C **Talk** with a partner. Practice the conversations. Pay attention to the stressed function words.

1. A We <u>don't</u> give refunds or exchanges on watches.
   B My warranty says you <u>can</u> if the merchandise is defective.
   A So, <u>is</u> it defective?
   B Yes, it <u>is</u>.
   A Then I <u>can</u> give you a refund.

2. A Who just mopped the floors, <u>you</u> or <u>Kevin</u>?
   B I did. <u>And</u> I cleaned the tables.
   A Good work. I <u>do</u> enjoy seeing a clean bakery.
   B And <u>I</u> love working here.

D Write two new conversations using stressed function words. Practice with a partner.

A *Does Karen need more help?*
B *No, but <u>I</u> do.*

LESSON A
Listening

1 **Before you listen**

A What do you see?

B What is happening?

Unit Goals
Identify environmental issues and concerns
Write a cause-and-effect paragraph about an environmental problem
Scan a chart to determine reasons to "live green"

2 Listen

STUDENT TK 31
CLASS CD2 TK 23

A **Listen** and answer the questions.

1. Who are the speakers?   2. What are they talking about?

STUDENT TK 31
CLASS CD2 TK 23

B **Listen again.** Complete the chart.

Ideas for living green	Will the family try?
1. *cut down on driving*	*No*
2.	
3.	
4.	
5.	
6.	

3 After you listen

A **Read.** Complete the story.

appliances	cut down on	environment	recycle
carpool	energy-efficient	global warming	responsibility

> Mei was late to dinner because she was looking at the Web site of The Living Green Council. "Living green" means taking <u>responsibility</u> for saving the earth from
> 1
> _____. Mei tells her parents about the guest speaker who came to her class.
> 2
> The speaker suggested simple things people could do to reduce their energy use and
> protect the _____. For example, they could _____ instead of driving
> 3   4
> alone, _____ their bottles and cans, and use _____ lightbulbs. Mei's
> 5   6
> parents agree that it is important to _____ energy use since it would also help
> 7
> them save money. However, they can't afford to buy new _____ right now.
> 8

STUDENT TK 32
CLASS CD2 TK 24

Listen and check your answers.

B **Discuss.** Talk with your classmates. Which of the speaker's suggestions can you try? Which are difficult for you? Why?

LESSON **B** Conditionals

1 Grammar focus: present unreal

would (100% sure)	*could* (less sure)
If everybody **drove** smaller cars, we **would use** less gasoline.	If she **wanted** to use less gasoline, she **could** probably **drive** a smaller car.
We **would use** less gasoline **if** everybody **drove** smaller cars.	She **could** probably **drive** a smaller car **if** she **wanted** to use less gasoline.

Turn to page 147 for a complete grammar chart and explanation.

2 Practice

A Write. Complete the sentences. Use the present unreal conditional.

1. Many people put their newspapers in the trash
   can. If everybody ___*recycled*___ newspapers, we
        (recycle)
   ___*would save*___ millions of trees.
        (save)

2. Noah never takes his car in for a tune-up.

   Noah's car _____ less gas if he _____
                  (use)   (tune up)
   his car regularly.

3. Mr. Brown drives his own car to his job downtown.

   I think Mr. Brown _____ money on gas if he
                          (save)
   _____ to work.
      (carpool)

4. Many items in the supermarket are packaged in plastic. If you _____ products
                                                                        (buy)
   that are packaged with recycled paper, you _____ to reduce global warming.
                                                    (help)

5. Jessica always stays in the shower for a very long time. If Jessica _____
                                                                              (take)
   shorter showers, she _____ water.
                            (save)

6. Some kinds of fish contain large amounts of lead, a poisonous metal. I think you

   _____ healthier if you _____ eating fish that contains lead.
        (be)   (stop)

Listen and check your answers.

B Talk with a partner. Match each action with a result. Some items have more than one correct answer. Use the present unreal conditional.

> If everybody bought energy-efficient appliances, we would save electricity.

Actions	Results
buy energy-efficient appliances	save gas
fix water leaks	cut down on energy use
replace lightbulbs with energy-efficient ones	save water
recycle cans, bottles, glass, and paper	reduce air-conditioning and heating use
put enough air in their tires	reduce the amount of trash in landfills
close off unused rooms	save electricity

Write sentences about the actions and results.

If everybody bought energy-efficient appliances, we would save electricity.

3 Communicate

A Work in a small group. Look at the picture of the beach. Talk about actions people could take to help the environment.

> If more people picked up the trash on the beach, everyone could enjoy a clean beach.

B Share ideas with your classmates.

☑ Use the present unreal conditional **UNIT 9** **113**

LESSON C Connectors

1 Grammar focus: *since* and *so*

Connector of cause

Since the earth is getting warmer, the polar ice caps are melting.

The polar ice caps are melting **since** the earth is getting warmer.

Connector of effect

The earth is getting warmer, **so** the polar ice caps are melting.

The earth is getting warmer, **so** the sea water is getting warmer.

Turn to page 147 for a grammar explanation.

> **USEFUL** LANGUAGE
>
> *Because* can replace *since*.
>
> *Therefore* can replace *so*.
>
> Use a semicolon before *therefore* and a comma after it.
>
> *The earth is getting warmer; therefore, the polar ice caps are melting.*

2 Practice

A Write. Combine the sentences. Use the connectors in parentheses.

1. There is a buildup of harmful gases in the atmosphere. Global warming is increasing. (since) *Since there is a buildup of harmful gases in the atmosphere, global warming is increasing.*

2. Warm water is expanding in the oceans. The sea level is rising. (so) *Warm water is expanding in the oceans, so the sea level is rising.*

3. The sea level is rising. Towns near oceans are in danger of flooding. (since) _____

4. Global warming changes weather patterns. Many places will have less rainfall. (because) _____

5. The mosquito population will increase. There will be an increase in diseases like malaria. (so) _____

6. The ocean water is getting warmer. Typhoons and hurricanes are becoming more frequent. (since) _____

7. Cities are growing. Many plants and animals may lose their natural habitats. (therefore) _____

 Listen and check your answers.

CLASS CD2 TK 26

B Talk with a partner. Combine sentences in different ways using the connectors *since*, *because*, *therefore*, and *so*.

> A Since people are building homes in forests, animals are losing their natural habitats.
> B Animals are losing their natural habitats because people are building homes in forests.

Causes	Effects
1. People are building homes in forests.	Animals are losing their natural habitats.
2. There is habitat loss.	Animals are moving into towns and cities.
3. Animals are moving into towns and cities.	The animals are frightened.
4. The animals are frightened.	Sometimes they attack people.
5. Wild animals sometimes attack people.	People are afraid of them.
6. People are afraid of wild animals.	They kill the animals.

Write sentences about the causes and effects.

Since people are building homes in forests, animals are losing their natural habitats.

3 Communicate

A Work in a small group. Read the newspaper headlines. Discuss the possible causes and effects of each event. Think of other possible headlines to discuss.

> Coyotes are losing their natural habitats, so they're moving into towns.

> Coyotes are moving into towns because they're losing their natural habitats.

THE MESSENGER
Another Coyote Moves into Town

THE NEWS
WHALE WASHES UP ON SHORE

THE DAILY
POLAR BEARS DROWNING AS ICE CAPS MELT

B Share information with your classmates.

☑ Use the connectors *since* and *because* to show cause and the connectors *so* and *therefore* to show effect

LESSON **D** Reading

1 Before you read

Talk with your classmates. Answer the questions.

1. What is a *fable*?
2. Do you know any fables or folktales from your native country? Which ones?

2 Read

Read the fable. Listen and read again.

STUDENT TK 33
CLASS CD2 TK 27

All Things Are Connected

Long ago, there was a village chief who never allowed anyone to disagree with him. Whenever he wanted to do something, he asked the members of his court for their advice. But whether the chief's idea was wise or foolish, his advisors always said the same thing, "Indeed, it is wise." Only one old woman dared to give a different answer. Whenever the chief asked for her advice, she always replied, "All things are connected."

One night, the chief was awakened by the sound of frogs croaking in the swamp. It happened again the next night and the next and the next. The chief decided to kill all the frogs in the swamp. When he consulted the members of his court, they replied as usual, "Indeed, it is wise." But the old woman kept silent. "And you, old woman, what do you think?" the chief demanded. "All things are connected," she replied. The chief concluded that the old woman was a fool, and he ordered his servants to kill all the frogs. Therefore, the chief slept peacefully.

But soon the mosquitoes in the swamp began to multiply since there were no frogs to eat them. They came into the village and made everyone miserable. The chief ordered his servants to go into the swamp and kill the mosquitoes, but it was impossible. Furious, the chief summoned the members of his court and blamed them, saying, "Why didn't you tell me that killing the frogs would make the mosquitoes multiply and everyone would be miserable? I should have listened to the old woman."

Because the mosquitoes were there, all the people of the village were forced to go away. Finally, the chief and his family left, too. Until he died, the chief never forgot the old woman's words, "All things are connected."

3 After you read

A Check your understanding.

1. Why couldn't the chief sleep?
2. What did he decide to do?
3. What did the members of his court say?
4. What did the old woman say?
5. What did the servants do?
6. What happened as a result?
7. Why was the chief furious?
8. Why did the people leave the village?
9. After reading the story, what does the title mean to you?

Ask yourself questions when you read to identify a cause-and-effect relationship.
- To find an effect, ask, "What happened?"
- To find a cause, ask, "Why did it happen?"

B Build your vocabulary.

1. In the reading passage, underline the words from the chart.
2. Use a dictionary or a thesaurus. Write the part of speech. Write an antonym for each word.

USEFUL LANGUAGE

An **antonym** is a word that has the opposite meaning.
good – bad
hard – easy
tall – short

Word	Part of speech	Antonym
wise	*adjective*	*foolish*
connected		
peacefully		
multiply		
miserable		
furious		
summoned		

3. Work in a small group. Write sentences with the words in the chart.

- _____
- _____
- _____

C Talk with a partner.

1. Do you think it is wise to follow other people's advice? Why or why not?
2. Give examples to show how plants and animals are connected.
3. How can people solve their conflicts peacefully?
4. What kind of weather makes you miserable?
5. What makes you furious?
6. What do you do when problems continue to multiply and you can't find solutions?
7. In what kinds of situations do people get summoned?

LESSON E Writing

1 Before you write

A **Talk** with a partner. Look at the picture. Answer the questions.

1. What is the environmental problem in this photo?
2. Why is it a problem? (causes)
3. How does this problem hurt people and the environment? (effects)

B **Read** the paragraph.

The Causes and Effects of Smog

Smog is a serious environmental problem in my city. One cause is that there are too many cars on the roads and highways. Most of the cars have only one person – the driver. People seem to take a lot of unnecessary trips. They drive to the drugstore instead of walking two blocks. Another cause of smog in my city is that we use too much electricity. Since many homes are not energy-efficient, our city's power plant has to produce more electricity. The burning coal from the power plant produces more air pollution. The smog is thick, so the air is hard to breathe. Consequently, on many days it is unsafe for children and senior citizens to be outside. Smog also kills many trees and plants that produce oxygen and clean the air. If people drove less and used less electricity, I am sure our air quality would improve.

One way to organize a paragraph is to discuss the causes and effects of a problem.

C **Work** with a partner. Complete the graphic organizer with information from the model paragraph.

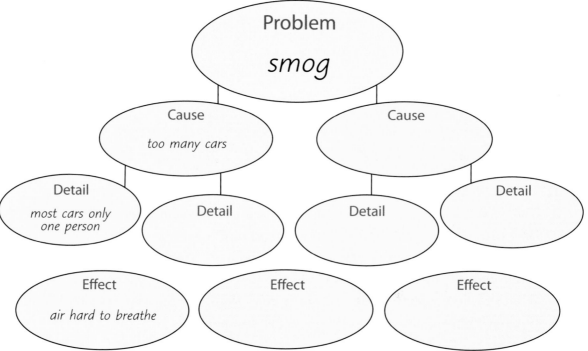

Problem

smog

Cause

too many cars

Cause

Detail

most cars only one person

Detail

Detail

Detail

Effect

air hard to breathe

Effect

Effect

D Plan a paragraph about an environmental problem in your city or community. Include the causes and effects of the problem. Use the graphic organizer to make notes on your ideas.

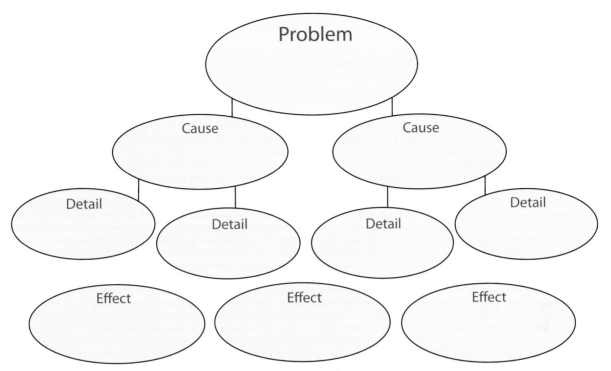

2 Write

Write a paragraph about an environmental problem in your city or community. Identify the problem in your topic sentence. Explain the causes and their effects and provide supporting details for each cause. Use the paragraph in Exercise 1B and the graphic organizers in Exercises 1C and 1D to help you.

3 After you write

A Check your writing.

	Yes	No
1. My topic sentence identifies an environmental problem.	☐	☐
2. I clearly explained the causes and effects.	☐	☐
3. I provided supporting details for the causes of the environmental problem.	☐	☐

B Share your writing with a partner.

1. Take turns. Read your paragraph to a partner.
2. Comment on your partner's paragraph. Ask your partner a question about the paragraph. Tell your partner one thing you learned.

LESSON F Another view

1 Life-skills reading

A Number of Reasons to Live Green

150	**400**	**1,000**
percent more energy is used by regular lightbulbs than energy-efficient (compact fluorescent) bulbs.	gallons of water are wasted every month when you have a leaky faucet.	years is how long plastic bottles take to decompose in landfills.
1,200	**95,000**	**14,000,000**
pounds of organic garbage are thrown out by the average American in a year.	pounds of pollution are produced by driving a car for one year.	trees are cut down to produce the 10,000,000,000 paper bags that Americans use every year.

A Read the questions. Look at the chart. Fill in the answer.

1. The chart does not discuss _____.

   Ⓐ plastic bottles in landfills

   Ⓑ pollution from cars

   Ⓒ pollution from airplanes

   Ⓓ cutting down trees to make bags

2. The number 400 represents _____.

   Ⓐ dollars

   Ⓑ gallons

   Ⓒ months

   Ⓓ days

3. What does the number 95,000 represent?

   Ⓐ pounds of organic garbage thrown out

   Ⓑ pounds of smog from factories

   Ⓒ pounds of pollution from a car in one year

   Ⓓ none of the above

4. How much organic garbage is thrown out each year by the average American?

   Ⓐ 21 pounds

   Ⓑ 200 pounds

   Ⓒ 1,200 pounds

   Ⓓ 95,000 pounds

5. How many paper bags do Americans use every year?

   Ⓐ 10,000,000

   Ⓑ 14,000,000

   Ⓒ 10,000,000,000

   Ⓓ 14,000,000,000

6. According to the chart, why are plastic bottles bad?

   Ⓐ Making them requires a lot of energy.

   Ⓑ They take a long time to decompose in landfills.

   Ⓒ They are expensive to make.

   Ⓓ none of the above

B Talk with your classmates. What do you do in your home to "live green"?

2 Grammar connections: present real conditional
vs. present unreal conditional

Use present real conditional when something is possible or always true.	Use present unreal conditional when something is not possible or not likely.
If I **have** time, I **walk** to school.	**If** I **found** a large bag of money, I **would give** it to charity.
If you **heat** water to 212° F, it **boils**.	**If** I **were** a bird, I'**d fly** all over the world.

A Work in a small group. Play the game. Write your name on a small piece of paper. Flip a coin to move your paper. Then tell your group about the topic in the square. Use the present real or present unreal conditional to finish the sentence. Take turns.

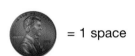 = 1 space

 = 2 spaces

> If I'm late to English class, I come in quietly.

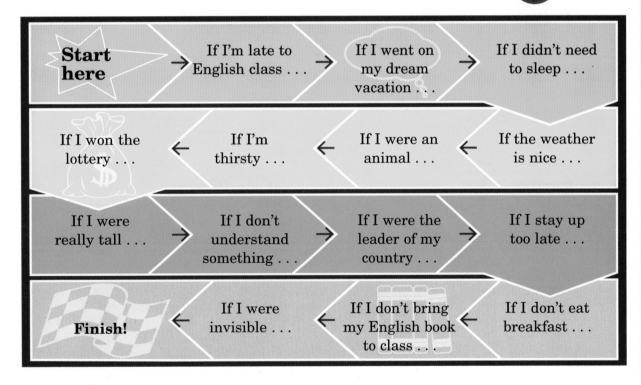

B Share information about your classmates.

> If Pedro is late to English class, he comes in quietly.

3 Wrap up

Complete the **Self-assessment** on page 140.

LESSON A
Listening

1 Before you listen

A What do you see?

B What is happening?

Unit Goals
Compare celebration customs
Read a recipe
Write about a favorite holiday

UNIT 10

2 Listen

STUDENT TK 34
CLASS CD2 TK 28

A **Listen** and answer the questions.

1. Who are the speakers?   2. What are they talking about?

STUDENT TK 34
CLASS CD2 TK 28

B **Listen again.** Complete the chart.

	American customs	**Vietnamese customs**
1. gifts	*register in a store*	
2. use of rice		
3. dress color		

3 After you listen

A **Read.** Complete the story.

acquaintances	fortune	reception	symbolizes
courses	looking forward	registered	tradition

Cathy and Thanh are talking about wedding customs. Cathy is invited to a Vietnamese wedding, and she is surprised that the bride and groom are not

___registered___ for gifts at any stores. In contrast, Thanh is surprised by the American
1

_____ of throwing rice at the bride and groom. Next, they talk about
2

clothes. Thanh says a Vietnamese bride wears a red dress because the color red

_____ good _____. Then Cathy asks why she was invited only to
3   4

the wedding _____, not the ceremony. Thanh explains that traditionally the
5

ceremony is only for the family. The couple's friends and _____ are invited
6

to the evening reception. In fact, Thanh says the evening party will include seven or

eight _____ of food. Cathy says she is _____ to the wedding.
7   8

STUDENT TK 35
CLASS CD2 TK 29

Listen and check your answers.

B **Discuss.** Talk with your classmates. Share some special wedding customs from your culture.

LESSON B Conditionals

1 Grammar focus: future real and present unreal

Future real (possible)	Present unreal (not possible)
If I **go** to the wedding, I **will wear** my new shoes.	**If** I **went** to the wedding, I **would wear** my new shoes. (But I'm not going.)
If Jane **doesn't have to work** on Saturday, she **will go** to the wedding.	**If** Jane **didn't have to work** on Saturday, she **would go** to the wedding. (But Jane has to work.)

Turn to page 147 for a grammar explanation.

2 Practice

Turn to page 147 for a grammar explanation.

> **USEFUL** LANGUAGE
>
> The present unreal conditional form of the verb *be* is *were*.
>
> *If I* ***were*** *you, I would give them cash for their wedding.*
>
> *If it* ***were*** *warmer, we could have the wedding outdoors.*

A Write. Complete the sentences. Use the future real or present unreal conditional forms of the verbs.

1. The Patels are from India, but they live in the United States now. They are planning a wedding for their daughter, Parveen. If they ___*lived*___ in India, (live) the groom's family ___*would pay*___ for the wedding. (pay)

2. The wedding will be in the United States. If the Patels _____ the wedding in India, the wedding (have) celebration _____ three days. Here it will last (last) for one day.

3. The Patels don't have a lot of money. If they _____ rich, they _____ (be) (invite) 300 people; instead, they will invite about 150.

4. The Patels are planning to have music for the reception. If a band _____ too (not / charge) much, they _____ live music. (have)

5. It's possible that the weather will be nice on the day of the wedding. If the weather _____ nice, they _____ the ceremony outside. (be) (have)

6. Parveen and her new husband will live in their own apartment. If they _____ (be) in India, they _____ with the groom's parents. (live)

 Listen and check your answers.

B Talk with a partner. Take turns making sentences about Victor's real and imaginary plans for New Year's Eve.

> **A** If Victor stays home on New Year's Eve, he will have a party with his friends.
> **B** But if he traveled to Florida, he would spend New Year's Eve near the beach.

Real	Imaginary
stay home / have a party with his friends	travel to Florida / spend New Year's Eve near the beach
go to his parents' house / have a quiet celebration with family	be in Mexico / eat 12 grapes at midnight
travel to New York / celebrate New Year's Eve in Times Square	travel to Brazil / watch fireworks on the beach at midnight
go to a club / dance all night	be in France / have a special dinner

Write sentences about Victor's real and imaginary plans.

If Victor stays home on New Year's Eve, he will have a party with his friends.

If he traveled to Florida, he would spend New Year's Eve near the beach.

3 Communicate

A Talk with a partner. Complete the chart with your real and imaginary plans for some future holidays or special events.

Holiday or event	Real	Imaginary
New Year's Eve	*stay home*	*be in my native country*
birthday		
(your idea)		
(your idea)		

B Work in a small group. Share your charts. Ask and answer questions about each other's plans.

> **A** If you stay home on New Year's Eve, how will you celebrate?
> **B** If I stay home, I'll invite my friends to come over and celebrate with me.

> **A** If you were in your native country on New Year's Eve, how would you celebrate?
> **B** If I were in my native country, I would watch fireworks at midnight.

C Share information about your classmates.

☑ Use future real and present unreal conditionals   **UNIT 10   125**

LESSON C *Hope* and *wish*

1 Grammar focus: possible and impossible

Possible situations	Situations that are not possible
Samira **hopes** her cousin **will come** to her wedding. Samira **hopes** her cousin **comes** to her wedding. Nick and Mia **hope** they **can go** to the party.	Samira **wishes** her cousin **would come** to her wedding. Nick and Mia **wish** they **could go** to the party.

Turn to page 148 for a grammar explanation.

USEFUL LANGUAGE

When expressing hopes, you can use the modal *will* or the simple present tense.

*I hope you **will attend**.*

*I hope you **attend**.*

2 Practice

A **Write.** Complete the sentences. Use *hope* or *wish* and the correct form of the verb or modal.

1. Paul's high school graduation is tomorrow.

   His friend Luis has to work. Luis ____*wishes*____ he

   ____*could go*____ to Paul's graduation.
   (can go)

2. Paul's father has asked for the day off so that he can

   attend his son's graduation. He _____ he

   _____ the day off.
   (get)

3. Paul's grandfather has been sick. He's not sure if he will

   attend the graduation. Paul _____ his grandfather _____ the ceremony.
   (will attend)

4. The graduation ceremony will be outside. Paul _____ it _____.
   (will not / rain)

5. Paul's parents would like to buy him a new car, but they can't afford it.

   They _____ they _____ him a new car.
   (can buy)

6. Paul wasn't accepted to the university, so he will go to a community college.

   Paul _____ he _____ to the university.
   (can go)

7. It's possible that Paul will be able to transfer to the university in two years.

   He _____ he _____ in two years.
   (can transfer)

 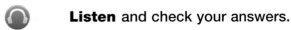 **Listen** and check your answers.

CLASS CD2 TK 31

B **Talk** with a partner. Read the situations. Make statements with *hope* or *wish*.

> Ryan wants to get a new cell phone soon.

> Ryan hopes he can get a new cell phone soon.

> Soraya can't go home for Thanksgiving.

> Soraya wishes she could go home for Thanksgiving.

1. Ryan wants to get a new cell phone soon.
2. Soraya can't go home for Thanksgiving because she has to work.
3. Marla wants to have a big graduation party, but her apartment is too small.
4. Avi is trying to get a plane reservation so he can attend his cousin's wedding in Las Vegas.
5. Karl plans to ask Marta to marry him next weekend. He doesn't know if she will say yes.
6. Maria wants to go to Spain, but she can't afford it.
7. Anton and Ilsa are expecting a baby. They want the baby to be healthy.

Write a sentence for each situation.

Ryan hopes he can get a new cell phone soon.

3 Communicate

A **Write** three holidays or celebrations that you observe. Think about something you wish you could change about each one.

    Mother's Day : *I wish I could have the day off to be with my children.*

1. _____ : _____

2. _____ : _____

3. _____ : _____

B **Work** in a small group. Talk about your wishes. Listen to your classmates' hopes for you.

> A I don't have Mother's Day off. I wish I could have the day off to be with my children.
> B I hope you get the day off next year.
> C I hope your children will do something special for you.

USEFUL LANGUAGE

Expressing hope is a common way of ending a conversation.
I hope you feel better soon.
I hope you have a good time.

C **Share** information about your classmates.

LESSON **D** Reading

1 Before you read

Talk with your classmates. Answer the questions.

1. How are birthdays usually celebrated in your culture?
2. Are some birthdays more special than others? Which ones?

2 Read

 Read the magazine article. Listen and read again.

STUDENT TK 36
CLASS CD2 TK 32

Special BIRTHDAYS Around the World

In most cultures, there are certain birthdays that are especially important in a young person's life. If you were an American teenager, for example, you would eagerly look forward to your 16th birthday because in most states that is the age to get a driver's license. Other cultures also have birthdays with special meanings:

A girl's Quinceañera

Mexico   For Mexican girls, the 15th birthday – the "Quinceañera" – symbolizes a girl's transition into adulthood. To celebrate, the girl's family throws a huge party. The girl wears a ball gown similar to a wedding dress. The girl performs a waltz, a formal dance, with her father. A similar custom is celebrated in Brazil.

China   On a child's first birthday, parents place their baby in the center of a group of objects, such as a shiny coin, a book, and a doll. Then they watch to see which object the baby picks up first. Most parents hope their child will pick up the coin because, according to tradition, it means the child will be rich.

Nigeria   The 1st, 5th, 10th, and 15th birthdays are considered extremely important. Parties are held with up to 100 people. The guests enjoy a feast of a roasted cow or goat.

Saudi Arabia   In some countries, such as Saudi Arabia, people don't observe birthdays at all because of spiritual beliefs. According to Muslim traditions, the only celebrations allowed are Eid al Fitr, a feast that signifies the end of Ramadan, and Eid al Adha, which celebrates the end of the annual pilgrimage to Mecca.

Israel   A boy's 13th and a girl's 12th birthdays are serious as well as happy occasions. On these birthdays, children become responsible for their own religious and moral behavior.

Adult birthdays also have special significance in many cultures. In the United States, for example, birthdays ending in "0" – 30, 40, 50, etc. – are especially meaningful.

3 After you read

A **Check** your understanding.

1. Why do American teenagers look forward to their 16th birthdays?
2. What is the Spanish word for a girl's 15th birthday?
3. What is a waltz?
4. Why are birthdays not celebrated in Saudi Arabia?
5. Which birthdays are especially meaningful in the United States?
6. Are any of the special birthdays described in the reading similar to traditions in your culture? Which ones?

> Punctuation can be a clue to meaning. For example, parentheses, commas, and dashes are all used to mark definitions, examples, or explanations.

B **Build** your vocabulary.

1. In the reading passage, underline the words from the chart. Write the meaning from the story.
2. Use a dictionary and write a different meaning for each word.

Word in story	Meaning in story	Other meaning
1. states	*areas that are part of a country*	*conditions of the mind*
2. object		
3. rich		
4. transition		
5. throw		
6. party		
7. ball		
8. pick up		
9. observe		

3. Write sentences using the other meaning of each word on your own paper.

C **Talk** with a partner.

1. How many states or provinces are there in your native country?
2. Do you have a favorite object? What is it? Why do you like it?
3. What transitions have you made in your life?
4. Have you ever thrown a large party? What was the occasion?
5. Have you ever attended a ball? If so, what did you wear?
6. What holidays do you observe?

☑ Recognize punctuation (parentheses, commas, and dashes) that signals definitions, examples, and explanations; use a dictionary to identify multiple meanings of a word **UNIT 10** **129**

LESSON E Writing

1 Before you write

A Talk with a partner.

1. Look at the pictures. Can you guess where the people are from and what holiday they are celebrating?
2. What is your favorite holiday or celebration? Why?

B Read the paragraph.

My Favorite Celebration

My favorite celebration is the Iranian New Year, *Norouz* ("new day"). This holiday begins on the first day of spring and lasts 13 days. On the Wednesday before Norouz, people build bonfires and jump over them. Iranian people believe that if they do this, they will get rid of their illnesses and misfortunes. On Norouz Eve, the family gathers around a table with seven items that begin with the letter "s" in Persian: an apple, wheat pudding, dried berries, vinegar, a coin, a beautiful flower, and garlic. A bowl of goldfish, a Koran, colored eggs, and a mirror are also on the table. These items symbolize beauty, health, prosperity, and fertility. On Norouz Day, people kiss each other and say, "I hope you will live for one hundred years." We spend the next 13 days visiting each other and eating sweets. Finally, on the last day of the celebration, everyone goes to a park for a big picnic. I wish my whole family lived with me here so that we could celebrate Norouz together.

> The conclusion – the last sentence of a paragraph – is an important part of a paragraph. One way to conclude a paragraph is to relate the topic to your personal life.

C Work with a partner. Complete the outline of the model paragraph.

I. Topic: _____*My Favorite Celebration - Norouz*_____

II. Meaning or symbolism: _____

_____

III. When celebrated: _____

IV. Customs:

    A. _____

    B. _____

    C. _____

    D. _____

    E. _____

V. Conclusion: _____

_____

D Plan a paragraph about your favorite holiday or celebration. Make an outline like the one in Exercise 1C. Include at least three customs. Use your own paper.

2 Write

Write a paragraph about your favorite holiday or celebration. Describe its meaning or symbolism. Include at least three customs. Write a conclusion that relates the celebration to your personal life. Use the paragraph in Exercise 1B and the outlines in Exercises 1C and 1D to help you.

3 After you write

A Check your writing.

	Yes	No
1. My paragraph describes the meaning or symbolism of my favorite holiday.	☐	☐
2. I described at least three customs for my favorite holiday or celebration.	☐	☐
3. I wrote a conclusion relating the celebration to my personal life.	☐	☐

B Share your writing with a partner.

1. Take turns. Read your paragraph to a partner.
2. Comment on your partner's paragraph. Ask your partner a question about the paragraph. Tell your partner one thing you learned.

LESSON F Another view

1 Life-skills reading

Mother's Thanksgiving Pumpkin Pie

Preparation time: 15 minutes / Cooking time: 50 minutes

Ingredients

1 pre-made pie crust
1 (8-ounce) package
  cream cheese, softened
2 cups canned pumpkin,
  mashed

¼ teaspoon salt
1 cup sugar
1 egg plus 2 egg yolks,
  lightly beaten
1 cup heavy cream

¼ cup (½ stick) melted butter
1 teaspoon vanilla extract
½ teaspoon ground cinnamon
¼ teaspoon ground ginger,
  optional

1. Preheat the oven to 350 degrees Fahrenheit.
2. Beat the softened cream cheese.
3. Add the pumpkin and beat until blended.
4. Then add the salt and sugar, and beat until blended.
5. Then add the egg mixed with the yolks, cream, and melted butter, and beat until blended.
6. Finally, mix in the vanilla, cinnamon, and ginger.

7. Pour the filling into the pre-made pie crust, and bake for 50 minutes, or until the center is firm.
8. Set the pie on a wire rack, and cool until it is room temperature. Cut into slices and serve with whipped cream or ice cream.

Serves 6–8 people.

A Read the questions. Look at the recipe. Fill in the answer.

1. How much sugar do you need to make the pie?
   - Ⓐ ¼ cup
   - Ⓑ ½ cup
   - Ⓒ 1 cup
   - Ⓓ 2 cups

2. What is the total cooking time for the pie?
   - Ⓐ 10 minutes
   - Ⓑ 15 minutes
   - Ⓒ 30 minutes
   - Ⓓ 50 minutes

3. Which ingredient do you need one cup of?
   - Ⓐ heavy cream
   - Ⓑ sugar
   - Ⓒ vanilla
   - Ⓓ both *a* and *b*

4. What should you do after you blend the cream cheese and pumpkin?
   - Ⓐ Add the salt and sugar.
   - Ⓑ Bake the pie.
   - Ⓒ Add the eggs.
   - Ⓓ Pour the filling into the pie crust.

5. How many people does this recipe serve?
   - Ⓐ 1–2
   - Ⓑ 3–4
   - Ⓒ 5–6
   - Ⓓ 6–8

6. Which ingredient is not required?
   - Ⓐ vanilla
   - Ⓑ ginger
   - Ⓒ cinnamon
   - Ⓓ cream cheese

B Talk with a partner. What is a traditional meal or recipe for a celebration in your culture? Describe the meal or recipe to your partner.

2 Grammar connections: tag questions

Affirmative sentence + negative tag	Negative sentence + affirmative tag
You **like** to dance, **don't** you? -Yes, I do. (I like to dance.) -Actually, no. I don't like to dance.	You **don't like** to dance, **do** you? -No, I don't. (I don't like to dance.) -Actually, yes. I like to dance.
You**'re** tired, **aren't** you?	You **aren't** tired, **are** you?
You **went** to a restaurant, **didn't** you?	You **didn't go** to a restaurant, **did** you?
You **were** absent, **weren't** you?	You **weren't** absent, **were** you?

A **Talk** with your classmates. Use tag questions. Complete the chart.

> A   Ivan, you don't like chocolate, do you?
> B   Actually, yes. I like chocolate.
> A   Fabiana, you don't like chocolate, do·you?
> C   No, I don't.

Find someone who . . .	Name
doesn't like chocolate	*Fabiana*
ate at a restaurant last night	
isn't tired today	
didn't go on vacation last month	
is good at math	
didn't study last night	
has a birthday in June	

B **Talk** with a partner. Ask questions about your partner's life. Use tag questions. Take turns.

> A   You like to fish, don't you?
> B   Yes, I do.

3 Wrap up

Complete the **Self-assessment** on page 140.

☑ Scan a recipe to get detail; use tag questions   **UNIT 10**   **133**

Review

1 Listening

CLASS CD2 TK 33

Listen. Take notes on a street interview.

Things that bring good luck	Things that bring bad luck
1. *wear bright colors like red*	4.
2.	5.
3.	6.

Talk with a partner. Check your answers.

2 Grammar

A Write. Complete the story.

A New Year's Eve Celebration

Sergei _____*wishes*_____ his friend Olga could visit him in New York over the
_____
1. hopes / wishes

holidays, but she can't get the time off. _____, they won't be together on
_____
2. Therefore / Since

New Year's Eve. If she _____ in New York, he would take her to Times
_____
3. is / were

Square _____ there is a big celebration there. Every year at one minute
_____
4. so / because

before midnight, a large crystal ball starts to drop slowly from high above the street. When it

reaches the bottom, everybody goes crazy _____ it's the beginning of the
_____
5. since / so

New Year. Sergei really _____ that Olga can come next year. If she comes,
_____
6. hopes / wishes

she _____ have a great time.
_____
7. will / would

B Write. Look at the words that are underlined in the answers. Write the questions.

1. **A** _____

   B Sergei would take Olga <u>to Times Square</u> if she were in New York.

2. **A** _____

   B <u>The crystal ball</u> starts to drop at one minute before midnight.

3. **A** _____

   B Sergei hopes that Olga can come <u>next year</u>.

Talk with a partner. Ask and answer the questions.

3 Pronunciation: linking consonant-vowel sounds

When a word ends in a consonant sound and the next word begins with a vowel sound, the words sound like they are linked together. Move the final consonant sound of the first word to the beginning of the second word.

CLASS CD2 TK 34

A **Listen** to the following sentences.

1. Smaller cars would use less energy.
2. Smog is a big environmental problem.
3. If everyone drove less, our air quality would improve.
4. In the future, we will see more electric cars and trucks on our roads.
5. We should all have efficient appliances.
6. We need to protect our environment.

Listen again and repeat. Pay attention to the linked consonant-vowel sounds.

CLASS CD2 TK 35

B **Listen and repeat.** Then underline the linked consonant-vowel sounds.

1. All things in this world are connected.
2. People are concerned about saving this earth.
3. Most of the cars on the highway have only one person in them.
4. People make a lot of unnecessary trips.
5. We should close off unused rooms in our homes.
6. The Internet is a good source of information about global warming.

Talk with a partner. Compare your answers.

C **Read** the questions and answers. Underline the linked consonant-vowel sounds.

1. A What do you think about global warming?

   B Well, I haven't read a lot about it.

2. A How can I help clean up the beach?

   B You can pick up trash and put it in garbage cans.

3. A What can all of us do to protect our environment?

   B We can all cut down on our energy use.

4. A What is an easy way to save energy?

   B Turn off lights when you leave a room.

Talk with a partner. Practice the questions and answers.

D **Write** four sentences from Units 9 and 10. Underline the linked consonant-vowel sounds. Then work with a partner. Read your sentences using linked consonant-vowel sounds.

Self-assessments

UNIT 1 Personal information

A **Vocabulary** Write eight new words you have learned.

_____ _____ _____ _____

_____ _____ _____ _____

B **Skills and functions** Read the sentences. Rate yourself. Circle 3 (*I agree.*) OR 2 (*I'm not sure.*) OR 1 (*I can't do this.*).

I can use nouns, verbs, adjectives, and adverbs: *He is a **good student**. He **reads quickly**.*	3 2 1
I can use noun clauses as objects: *I believe **that every person is unique**.*	3 2 1
I can use **so** and **that** in questions and answers: *Do you think **that** the unemployment rate will go down? Yes, I hope **so**.*	3 2 1
I can skim an article to get a general idea of what it is about.	3 2 1
I can write a paragraph with a topic sentence and supporting sentences.	3 2 1

C **What's next?** Choose one.

☐ I am ready for the unit test.   ☐ I need more practice with _____.

UNIT 2 At school

A **Vocabulary** Write eight new words you have learned.

_____ _____ _____ _____

_____ _____ _____ _____

B **Skills and functions** Read the sentences. Rate yourself. Circle 3 (*I agree.*) OR 2 (*I'm not sure.*) OR 1 (*I can't do this.*).

I can ask and answer questions with the present passive: ***Are** internships **offered** for this program? Yes, internships **are offered**.*	3 2 1
I can use infinitives after the passive: *The student **is required to take** a placement test.*	3 2 1
I can use **be supposed to** and **be not supposed to** to show expectations: *You're **supposed to walk** at the swimming pool. You're **not supposed to run**.*	3 2 1
I can scan an article to find specific information.	3 2 1
I can write a paragraph using specific details such as facts, examples, and reasons to support my topic sentence.	3 2 1

C **What's next?** Choose one.

☐ I am ready for the unit test.   ☐ I need more practice with _____.

UNIT 3 Friends and family

A **Vocabulary** Write eight new words you have learned.

_____   _____   _____   _____

_____   _____   _____   _____

B **Skills and functions** Read the sentences. Rate yourself. Circle 3 (*I agree.*) OR
2 (*I'm not sure.*) OR 1 (*I can't do this.*).

I can ask indirect *Wh-* questions: *I'd like to know **why Ana is** so strict. Can you tell me **why Ana is** so strict?*	3 2 1
I can ask indirect *Yes / No* questions: *I'd like to know **if you finished** your homework. Can you tell me **whether you finished** your homework?*	3 2 1
I can use **say** and **tell** with reported speech: *Joshua **said** he has a sister. Joshua **told me** he has a sister.*	3 2 1
I can recognize words that are repeated to get an idea of what a reading is about.	3 2 1
I can write a paragraph using transition words that show the relationship between sentences or ideas within a paragraph.	3 2 1

C **What's next?** Choose one.

☐ I am ready for the unit test.   ☐ I need more practice with _____.

UNIT 4 Health

A **Vocabulary** Write eight new words you have learned.

_____   _____   _____   _____

_____   _____   _____   _____

B **Skills and functions** Read the sentences. Rate yourself. Circle 3 (*I agree.*) OR
2 (*I'm not sure.*) OR 1 (*I can't do this.*).

I can make sentences with **should**, **shouldn't**, **have to**, and **don't have to** to express advice, necessity, or lack of necessity: *You **should call** her.*	3 2 1
I can use **should have** and **shouldn't have** to talk about regrets and advice in the past: *I **should have gone** to school today. I **shouldn't have stayed** home.*	3 2 1
I can use **may, might**, and **must** to talk about degrees of certainty: *Phana took the bus today. Her car **must be** broken. It **might have** a flat tire.*	3 2 1
I can relate the title and section heads of a text to my own experience.	3 2 1
I can write a paragraph organized by cause and effect.	3 2 1

C **What's next?** Choose one.

☐ I am ready for the unit test.   ☐ I need more practice with _____.

UNIT 5 Around town

A | **Vocabulary** Write eight new words you have learned.

_____ _____ _____ _____

_____ _____ _____ _____

B | **Skills and functions** Read the sentences. Rate yourself. Circle 3 (*I agree.*) OR 2 (*I'm not sure.*) OR 1 (*I can't do this.*).

I can make sentences with future time clauses using **until** and **as soon as**: *She stayed **until** he finished lunch. She left **as soon as** he finished lunch.*	3 2 1
I can use the correct verb tense to talk about repeated actions in the present and past: *She **volunteers** three times a month. She **has volunteered** twice this month.*	3 2 1
I can distinguish between **used to** and **be used to**: *I **used to live** in a large city. I **am not used to driving** everywhere.*	3 2 1
I can guess if a word is positive or negative by reading the words around it.	3 2 1
I can write a paragraph with details answering *Wh-* questions.	3 2 1

C | **What's next?** Choose one.

☐ I am ready for the unit test.   ☐ I need more practice with _____.

UNIT 6 Time

A | **Vocabulary** Write eight new words you have learned.

_____ _____ _____ _____

_____ _____ _____ _____

B | **Skills and functions** Read the sentences. Rate yourself. Circle 3 (*I agree.*) OR 2 (*I'm not sure.*) OR 1 (*I can't do this.*).

I can make sentences with **although** and **even though**: *I drive **although** the subway is cheaper. I drive **even though** the subway is cheaper.*	3 2 1
I can distinguish between **because** and **although**: *I drive **because** it is convenient. I drive **although** gas is expensive.*	3 2 1
I can use **so** + adjective and **such** + adjective + noun: *That computer is **so old**. That's **such an old computer**.*	3 2 1
I can distinguish between fact and opinion.	3 2 1
I can write a paragraph describing advantages and disadvantages.	3 2 1

C | **What's next?** Choose one.

☐ I am ready for the unit test.   ☐ I need more practice with _____.

UNIT 7 Shopping

A **Vocabulary** Write eight new words you have learned.

_____ _____ _____ _____

_____ _____ _____ _____

B **Skills and functions** Read the sentences. Rate yourself. Circle 3 (*I agree.*) OR 2 (*I'm not sure.*) OR 1 (*I can't do this.*).

I can use subject-pattern adjective clauses: *I want to get a camera **that's not too expensive**.*	3 2 1
I can use object-pattern adjective clauses: *I like the car **that you bought**.*	3 2 1
I can use clarification questions to get more information: *I went to school. You went **where**?*	3 2 1
I can recognize synonyms in a reading.	3 2 1
I can write a paragraph using transition words to signal a list of reasons.	3 2 1

C **What's next?** Choose one.

☐ I am ready for the unit test.   ☐ I need more practice with _____.

UNIT 8 Work

A **Vocabulary** Write eight new words you have learned.

_____ _____ _____ _____

_____ _____ _____ _____

B **Skills and functions** Read the sentences. Rate yourself. Circle 3 (*I agree.*) OR 2 (*I'm not sure.*) OR 1 (*I can't do this.*).

I can distinguish between the present perfect and present perfect continuous: *He **has talked** to the manager. He **has been talking** to the manager for several minutes.*	3 2 1
I can use adjectives ending in *-ed* and *-ing* to describe feelings or characteristics: *She's **excited**. The job is **exciting**.*	3 2 1
I can make polite requests and offers: ***Would you open** the door? **Let me open** the door for you.*	3 2 1
I can recognize quotations and reasons for using them.	3 2 1
I can write a cover letter that includes information about skills and experience.	3 2 1

C **What's next?** Choose one.

☐ I am ready for the unit test.   ☐ I need more practice with _____.

UNIT 9 Daily living

A **Vocabulary** Write eight new words you have learned.

_____ _____ _____ _____

_____ _____ _____ _____

B **Skills and functions** Read the sentences. Rate yourself. Circle 3 (*I agree.*) OR 2 (*I'm not sure.*) OR 1 (*I can't do this.*).

I can make sentences using the present unreal conditional: **If** everybody **drove** smaller cars, we **would use** less gasoline.	3 2 1	
I can use **since**, **so**, **because**, and **therefore** to show cause and effect: **Since** the earth is getting warmer, the polar ice caps are melting. The earth is getting warmer. **Therefore**, the polar ice caps are melting.	3 2 1	
I can distinguish between present real and present unreal conditionals: **If I have** time, I **walk** to school. **If I found** a bag of money, I **would give** it to charity.	3 2 1	
I can ask myself questions when I read to identify a cause-and-effect relationship.	3 2 1	
I can write a paragraph describing the causes and effects of a problem.	3 2 1	

C **What's next?** Choose one.

☐ I am ready for the unit test.   ☐ I need more practice with _____.

UNIT 10 Free time

A **Vocabulary** Write eight new words you have learned.

_____ _____ _____ _____

_____ _____ _____ _____

B **Skills and functions** Read the sentences. Rate yourself. Circle 3 (*I agree.*) OR 2 (*I'm not sure.*) OR 1 (*I can't do this.*).

I can distinguish between future real and present unreal conditionals: **If I have** time, I **will call** you. **If I had** more time, I **would call** you.	3 2 1	
I can make statements using **hope** and **wish**: **I hope** I can come to the party. **I wish** I could come to the party.	3 2 1	
I can make sentences using tag questions: You're tired, **aren't you**? You weren't absent, **were you**?	3 2 1	
I can recognize punctuation in a reading that gives a clue to meaning.	3 2 1	
I can write a conclusion that relates the topic to my personal life.	3 2 1	

C **What's next?** Choose one.

☐ I am ready for the unit test.   ☐ I need more practice with _____.

Reference

Nouns, verbs, adjectives, adverbs

Adjectives give information about *nouns*.
Adverbs give information about *verbs*. Most adverbs end in *-ly*.
Adverbs that describe how something happens are called *adverbs of manner*.
A few adverbs are irregular, such as *fast*, *well*, and *hard*.

Adjective + noun

Carol is an *intelligent* girl.

Verb + regular adverb

Carol speaks *intelligently*.

Verb + irregular adverb

Carol speaks *well*.

Sometimes the same word can be an adjective or an adverb.

Adjective

It's a *hard* test. John is a *fast* worker.

Adverb

John works *hard* and *fast*.

Clauses

A *clause* is a part of a sentence that has a subject and a verb.
A *main clause* is a complete sentence.
A *dependent clause* is not a complete sentence; it is connected to a main clause.
A sentence with the structure main clause + dependent clause or dependent clause + main clause is called a *complex sentence*.

that clauses as objects

Some complex sentences have the form main clause + noun clause (see *Clauses* above).
A noun clause is a type of dependent clause. Some noun clauses have the form *that* + subject + verb.
However, it is also correct to omit *that*. The main clause can be a statement or a question.

	Main clause	**Noun clause**
Statement	People think	(that) she is smart.
Question	Do you think	(that) she is smart?

Present passive

Active sentences have the form subject + verb + object. Passive sentences have the form subject + *be* + past participle. The object of an active sentence becomes the subject of a passive sentence. An active verb is used to say what the subject does. A passive verb is used to say what happens to the subject. A passive sentence is most common when the person or thing that does the action is not important. If the passive is used, and it is important to know who performs an action, a phrase consisting of *by* + noun comes after the passive verb. More often, the passive is used without the *by* phrase.
See page 149 for a list of irregular past participles.

Affirmative statements

Active		Passive
The college gives an English placement test twice a year.	**Singular**	An English placement test is given (by the college) twice a year.
The college offers online classes every semester.	**Plural**	Online classes are offered every semester (by the college).

Yes / No questions

Active		Passive
Does the college offer financial aid?	**Singular**	Is financial aid offered (by the college)?
Does the college give online courses every semester?	**Plural**	Are online courses given every semester (by the college)?

Wh- questions

Active		Passive
When does the college give the placement test?	**Singular**	When is the placement test given (by the college)?
Where does the college hold English classes?	**Plural**	Where are English classes held (by the college)?

Infinitives after passive verbs

Some passive verbs can have an infinitive after them.

Active	Passive
The teacher tells the students to bring a dictionary to class.	The students are told to bring a dictionary to class.

Verbs infinitives often follow

advise	intend	require
allow	mean	tell
encourage	plan	use
expect	prepare	

Direct and indirect questions

A *direct* question is a complete sentence. An *indirect* question contains a main clause and a dependent clause (see *Clauses* on page 141). The main clause can be a statement or a question. If it is a question, a question mark is used at the end of the sentence. The dependent clause in indirect *Wh-* questions begins with a question word (*who, what, where, when, why,* or *how*). The dependent clause in indirect *Yes / No* questions begins with *if* or *whether*. *Whether* is more formal.

Wh- questions

	Direct	Indirect
Present	When does the bus come?	Do you know when the bus comes?
Past	Where did she go?	Please tell me where she went.

Yes / No questions

	Direct	Indirect
Present	Do they have a test today?	Do you know if they have a test today? Do you know whether they have a test today?
Past	Did he finish his homework?	I wonder if he finished his homework. I'd like to know whether he finished his homework.

Common introductory clauses that are used with indirect questions

I'd like to know . . .	I wonder . . .	Do you have any idea . . . ?
I don't know . . .	Please explain . . .	Can you tell me . . . ?
I want to know . . .	Tell me . . .	Do you know . . . ?
I need to know . . .		

Present modals: *should, shouldn't, ought to, have to, don't have to*

Ought to is the same as *should*. It is used to give advice. *Shouldn't* is the opposite of both *ought to* and *should*. *Have to / Has to* mean that it is necessary to do something. The subject has no choice about it. *Don't have to / Doesn't have to* mean that it is not necessary to do something. The subject can choose to do it or not.

Affirmative statements

I		
You	should ought to have to	relax.
We		
They		
He	should ought to has to	relax.
She		
It		

Negative statements

I		
You	shouldn't don't have to	work so hard.
We		
They		
He	shouldn't doesn't have to	work so hard.
She		
It		

Past modals: *should have, shouldn't have*

Should have / shouldn't have + past participle mean that the speaker is sorry about (regrets) something he or she did or did not do in the past. These modals can also be used to give advice about something in the past.

Affirmative statements

I		
You		
We		
They	should have	left earlier.
He		
She		
It		

Negative statements

I		
You		
We		
They	shouldn't have	arrived late.
He		
She		
It		

Time clauses with *until* and *as soon as*

Dependent time clauses with *until* and *as soon as* can come at the beginning or end of a sentence.
Use *until* in the dependent clause to say how long an action continues.
Use *as soon as* in the dependent clause to mean "right after."
Use a comma (,) after a time clause when it comes at the beginning of a sentence.

until	*Until* the patient finished his lunch, the nurse stayed with him. The nurse stayed with the patient *until* he finished his lunch.
as soon as	*As soon as* the patient finished his lunch, the nurse left. The nurse left *as soon as* the patient finished his lunch.

Time words and expressions to describe repeated actions

In sentences that talk about repeated actions in the present or past, the correct word order is subject + verb + number of times + time expression.

		Number of times	Time expressions
Present	This year, Sana volunteers at the shelter This year, Sana is volunteering	once twice three times several times many times	a week. each month.
Past	In 2011, Sana volunteered		each month. last year. two years ago. when she was 12.
Present perfect	Sana has volunteered		so far. in her life.

Concession clauses with *although* and *even though*

Although and *even though* introduce dependent clauses of concession. Concession clauses give information that is surprising or unexpected compared to the information in the main clause. Concession clauses can come at the beginning or end of a sentence. Use a comma (,) after a concession clause when it comes at the beginning of a sentence. Usually you can use *but* or *however* to rephrase a sentence with *although* or *even though*, but the grammar is different.

although / *even though*	*Although / Even though* e-mail is convenient, Mr. Chung doesn't like to use it. Mr. Chung doesn't like to use e-mail *although / even though* it is convenient.
but	E-mail is convenient, *but* Mr. Chung doesn't like to use it.
however	E-mail is convenient. *However*, Mr. Chung doesn't like to use it.

Clauses of reason

Because introduces a dependent clause of reason, which gives reasons for information in the main clause. Clauses of reason can come at the beginning or end of a sentence. Use a comma (,) after a clause of reason when it comes at the beginning of a sentence.

Because wireless technology is fast, many people use it.
Many people use wireless technology *because* it is fast.

Adjective clauses with *who* and *that*

An adjective clause comes after a noun. The noun can be in the middle or at the end of the sentence. It can be a person or a thing. *Who* and *that* are used to describe people. *That* and *which* are used to describe things. There are two kinds of adjective clauses: *subject pattern* and *object pattern*.

Subject-pattern adjective clauses

The adjective clause has the form *who*, *that*, or *which* + verb.
Who, *that*, or *which* is the subject of the adjective clause.

A camera *that is on sale* costs $99.
I want to buy a camera *that costs less than $100*.

The salesperson *who helped me* gave me good advice.
The salesperson *that helped me* gave me good advice.

Object-pattern adjective clauses

The adjective clause has the form *that* + noun or pronoun + verb.
That is the object of the adjective clause. In object-pattern adjective clauses you can omit *that*.

I like the car *that you bought*.
I like the car *you bought*.

The mechanic *that I use* has a lot of experience.
The mechanic *I use* has a lot of experience.

Present perfect

The present perfect is formed by *have / has* + past participle. One of the uses of the present perfect is to talk about recently finished actions (with or without *just*).
See page 149 for a list of irregular past participles.

Affirmative statements

I		
You	have (just)	
We		cleaned the windows.
They		
He	has (just)	
She		
It	has (just)	stopped raining.

Present perfect continuous

The present perfect continuous is formed by *have / has* + *been* + verb *-ing*. Use the present perfect continuous to talk about actions that started in the past, continue to now, and may continue in the future. Use *for* + length of time or *since* + specific time to give the meaning of *how long*.

Affirmative statements

I		
You	have been working	
We		for an hour.
They		since 8:00.
He	has been working	
She		
It		

With verbs that are not actions (e.g., *have*, *be*, *know*), use the present perfect with *for* or *since*: *I have known him for two years. I have known him since 2012.*
With some action verbs, you can use either the present perfect or the present perfect continuous with *for* or *since*: *I have studied / been studying here for six months.*

Participial adjectives

Verb forms that end in *-ed* or *-ing* are called *participles*. Participles can be adjectives. There is a difference in meaning between the *-ed* and *-ing* forms. Often, the *-ing* form describes a thing or person, and the *-ed* form describes the way someone feels.

Affirmative statements

John's job is very *tiring*. At the end of the day, he is always *tired*.
Mary is at the movies. She is *bored* because the movie is very *boring*.

Conditionals

Conditional sentences have a dependent clause and a main clause. The dependent clause begins with *if*. The *if* clause can come at the beginning or end of a sentence. Use a comma (,) after an *if* clause when it comes at the beginning of a sentence. Conditional sentences can be real or unreal. "Real" means the situation in the sentence is possible. "Unreal" means the situation isn't possible; it is imaginary. In unreal conditional sentences, the form of the *be* verb in the dependent clause is *were* for all persons, but in informal situations people use *I was*. The clause *if I were you* is used for giving advice.

Present real conditional

Dependent clause	Main clause	Example
if + subject + present verb	subject + present verb	If you *heat* water to 212° F, it *boils*. Water *boils* if you *heat* it to 212° F.

Future real conditional

Dependent clause	Main clause	Example
if + subject + present verb	subject + future verb	If I *have* time, I *will bake* a cake. I *will bake* a cake if I *have* time.

Present unreal conditional

Dependent clause	Main clause	Example
if + subject + past verb	subject + *would / could / might* + base form of verb	If I *had* time, I *would bake* a cake. I *would bake* a cake if I *had* time.
if + subject + *were*	subject + *would / could / might* + base form of verb	If I *were* you, I *would give* Maria a gift card for her birthday. I *would give* Maria a gift card for her birthday if I *were* you.

Connectors of cause and effect

English has many words and phrases to signal cause (reason) and effect (result). Although the meanings of these words and phrases are similar, their form is different.

since and *because*	Use these words in dependent clauses to signal the cause. Use a comma (,) when the dependent clause is at the beginning of a sentence. *Since / Because* the earth is getting warmer, the sea level is rising. The sea level is rising *since / because* the earth is getting warmer.
so and *therefore*	These words signal an effect. They come at the beginning of a main clause. They are followed by a comma. The earth is getting warmer. *So / Therefore*, the sea level is rising.

hope and *wish*

Use *hope* to talk about something you want in the future that is possible. Use *wish* to talk about situations that are not possible (imaginary). Both *hope* and *wish* occur in main clauses and are followed by dependent *that* clauses (see *that* clauses as objects on page 141).

hope	The dependent clause has a present or future verb or modal. I *hope* (that) you *can come* to my wedding. Sandor *hopes* (that) his son *will fly* home for Thanksgiving.
wish	The dependent clause has a past verb or *would / could* + base form of the verb. I *wish* (that) you *could come* to my wedding. Sandor *wishes* (that) his son *would fly* home for Thanksgiving.

Spelling rules

Spelling rules for gerunds

- For verbs ending in a vowel-consonant pair, repeat the consonant before adding *-ing*:

  stop → stopping   *get → getting*

- For verbs ending in a silent *-e,* drop the *e* before adding *-ing*:

  dance → dancing   *exercise → exercising*

  but:

  be → being   *see → seeing*

Spelling rules for regular past participles

- To form the past participle of regular verbs, add *-ed* to the base form:
  listen → listened

- For regular verbs ending in a consonant + *-y*, change *y* to *i* and add *-ed*:
  study → studied

- For regular verbs ending in a vowel + *-y*, add *-ed*:
  play → played

- For regular verbs ending in *-e*, add *-d*:
  live → lived

Capitalization rules

Capitalize adjectives that are made from the names of places.	**M**exican girls **I**ranian holiday **A**merican dream
Capitalize important words in titles, but not prepositions or the second part of a hyphenated word.	**S**tory **L**ady **R**unning with **R**opes **M**y **F**avorite **T**ime-saving **D**evice

Irregular verbs

Base form	Simple past	Past participle	Base form	Simple past	Past participle
be	was / were	been	lose	lost	lost
become	became	become	make	made	made
begin	began	begun	meet	met	met
break	broke	broken	oversleep	overslept	overslept
bring	brought	brought	pay	paid	paid
build	built	built	put	put	put
buy	bought	bought	read	read	read
catch	caught	caught	ride	rode	ridden
choose	chose	chosen	run	ran	run
come	came	come	say	said	said
cost	cost	cost	see	saw	seen
cut	cut	cut	sell	sold	sold
do	did	done	send	sent	sent
drink	drank	drunk	set	set	set
drive	drove	driven	show	showed	shown
eat	ate	eaten	sing	sang	sung
fall	fell	fallen	sit	sat	sat
feel	felt	felt	sleep	slept	slept
fight	fought	fought	speak	spoke	spoken
find	found	found	spend	spent	spent
fly	flew	flown	stand	stood	stood
forget	forgot	forgotten	steal	stole	stolen
get	got	gotten / got	swim	swam	swum
give	gave	given	take	took	taken
go	went	gone	teach	taught	taught
have	had	had	tell	told	told
hear	heard	heard	think	thought	thought
hide	hid	hidden	throw	threw	thrown
hit	hit	hit	understand	understood	understood
hold	held	held	wake	woke	woken
hurt	hurt	hurt	wear	wore	worn
keep	kept	kept	win	won	won
know	knew	known	write	wrote	written
leave	left	left			

Self-study audio script

Welcome

Page 3, Exercise 2A – Track 2

A Hi, Mark. I see you're studying for the vocabulary test. You did so well on the last one. What's your secret?

B I make vocabulary cards. I write the vocabulary words on one side of the card and then write the definition on the other side. I also write an example sentence with the word in it and draw a picture for some words. I test myself and ask others to test me, too.

A Oh, that's a creative way to study, and I can see that you're artistic, too.

B Thanks! And you always do well on math tests. What strategies do you use for studying math?

A I like to study with other people. We form a small group and test each other on equations and formulas. We have fun while we study so the time goes by fast.

B You're so outgoing and fun-loving – I can see how that fits your personality. Who do you study with?

A I often study with Juan. He's an active person and likes to study while moving – sometimes we memorize formulas while bouncing a basketball. It's a good way to remember something.

Page 4, Exercise 3A – Track 3

1. Mohammed was listening to the radio.
2. Yoko heard a loud noise.
3. Last night at 8:00 p.m., the Martinez family was watching television.
4. I woke up at 6:00 a.m. this morning.
5. Merin was playing her violin this morning.
6. Isabella and Jeremy were doing their homework.
7. Marcos drove to the supermarket.
8. Nur vacuumed the house yesterday.

Page 4, Exercise 3B – Track 4

Last summer, my sister and I drove from Tucson to Phoenix. On our way, it was very windy, and there were dark clouds in the sky. We were traveling slowly when suddenly we saw huge clouds of dust in the air. The sky turned brown, and we couldn't see anything. It was very scary.

While we were driving, we were looking for a place to turn off the road. Finally we came to an exit and got off the main road. We went into a restaurant. The dust finally went away while we were waiting at the restaurant.

Page 5, Exercise 4A – Track 5

1. I went to Niagara Falls with my family last year.
2. Angelica hasn't been to Mexico City.
3. Claudia and Paul have never gone camping before.

4. Sabina volunteered at the Humane Society last year.
5. Have you ever cooked Korean food?
6. My father was a very confident person.
7. Peter enjoyed socializing with other people.
8. Roberta has traveled all over the world.
9. Monica has learned several languages.
10. Has Manuel ever taken English classes?

Page 5, Exercise 4B – Track 6

1. **A** Have you ever practiced English with a conversation partner?
   B No, I haven't. I'm too shy.
2. **A** Did you go to the theater last night?
   B Yes, I did. The movie was great.
3. **A** Have you ever gone dancing in a night club?
   B No, I haven't. I'm not very outgoing.
4. **A** Did Daniel volunteer at the elementary school yesterday?
   B Yes, he did. He is very reliable.
5. **A** Has your son ever been in a school play?
   B Yes, he has. He's very enthusiastic about acting.

Unit 1: Personal information

Page 7, Exercises 2A and 2B – Track 7

A Come on in. The door's open!

B Hi, Nina!

A Emily! Come on in. Have you been jogging?

B Yeah, I was just coming back from my run, and I thought I'd see what you're – whoa! Look at this kitchen!

A Yeah, it's a mess, isn't it? We're having 14 people for dinner tonight, and I'm going to be in the kitchen all afternoon!

B It smells great already! Hey, I just heard that Brenda got first place in the high school math contest. Is it true?

A Yes, it's true! She's really good at math. She just loves it.

B Brenda's such a "brain." I'm sure you're really proud of her!

A Yeah, she's very intelligent. But I have to say that Gerry and Danny are bright, too – they're just smart in different ways.

B What do you mean?

A Well, take Gerry. He's not mathematical like Brenda, but he's really musical. He plays four different instruments, he sings really well – he's even writing some of his own songs.

B I guess that's Gerry!

A Yeah.

B So Brenda's gifted in math, and Gerry's good at music. What about Danny? What's he good at?

A Well, he's good at fixing cars. He's the mechanical one in the family.

B Oh, I remember he bought that old, old car when he was 16. How's that coming? Is he still working on it?

A Emily, you should see that car now! It's gorgeous! He fixed everything, and it runs perfectly!

B Amazing! You know, it's really interesting how your kids are all smart in different ways. And, Nina, you're pretty smart, too!

A Me?

B Well, look at you! Maybe it's easy for you to cook for 14 people, but I could never do it. I have absolutely no aptitude for cooking!

A Gee, Emily. No one ever told me that I'm smart!

B Well, Nina, you are smart! And the smart thing for me to do is to go home and let you do your work. I'll talk to you tomorrow.

A Bye, Emily. Thanks for stopping by!

Page 7, Exercise 3A – Track 8

Emily stops by Nina's house on her way home from jogging. They talk about Nina's three children. Brenda is very mathematical. She's just won a math contest at school. When Emily calls Brenda a brain, Nina says that all her children are bright, but in different ways. Gerry isn't gifted in math, but he's very musical. He plays and sings very well and even writes music. Danny is the mechanical one in the family. He's good at fixing up old cars. Emily thinks that Nina is also smart because she is such a good cook. Emily has no aptitude for cooking.

Page 12, Exercise 2 – Track 9

Many Ways to Be Smart

Josh is a star on the school baseball team. He gets Ds and Fs on all his math tests. His brother, Frank, can't catch, throw, or hit a baseball, but he easily gets As in math. Which boy do you think is more intelligent? Howard Gardner, a professor of education at Harvard University, would say that Josh and Frank are both smart, but in different ways. His theory of multiple intelligences identifies eight different "intelligences" to explain the way people understand, experience, and learn about the world around them.

Verbal / Linguistic Some people are good with words. They prefer to learn by reading, listening, and speaking.

Logical / Mathematical These people have an aptitude for math. They like solving logic problems and puzzles.

Musical / Rhythmical These people are sensitive to sound, melodies, and rhythms. They are gifted in singing, playing instruments, or composing music.

Visual / Spatial These "picture people" are often good at drawing or painting. They are sensitive to colors and designs.

Bodily / Kinesthetic Some people are "body smart." They are often athletic. Kinesthetic learners learn best when they are moving.

Interpersonal Certain people are "group smart." They easily understand other people. They are good at communicating and interacting with others.

Intrapersonal Some people are "self smart." They can understand their own feelings and emotions. They often enjoy spending time alone.

Naturalist These people are skilled in working with plants and animals in the natural world.

According to Gardner, many people have several or even all of these intelligences, but most of us have one or two intelligences that are primary, or strongest.

Unit 2: At school

Page 19, Exercises 2A and 2B – Track 10

Part 1

Do you like to work with people? Do you enjoy traveling? Are you bilingual? Then La Costa Community College's Hospitality and Tourism certificate program is for you. Our graduates find high-paying jobs with hotels, restaurants, airlines, travel agencies, and more! This growing industry needs leaders – it needs you! For more information about La Costa's certificate program in Hospitality and Tourism, call 866-555-6868 today!

Part 2

A Mrs. Ochoa?
B Oh, hi, Vasili. How's it going?
A Pretty well. Um, I was in my car this morning, and I heard an advertisement about a certificate program in hospitality and tourism.
B Yes, it's a great program. Are you interested?
A Yeah, but I have some questions.
B Well, I'll try to answer them for you.
A OK. So first, what are the requirements for the certificate? How many courses are required?
B There are six required courses, plus an internship.
A An internship? What's that?
B You work at a local tourism business for three months. There's no pay, but it's a great way to learn about the industry – you know, see if you like it.
A I see. Are the classes in the daytime or at night? Because you know, I can't quit my job, and . . .
B No problem, Vasili. Classes are scheduled at different times, and some of them are even offered online.

A Oh, yeah? That's great. Um, how long does it take to complete the program?
B Well, it depends. I'd say – with the internship – between one and two years. Some people just take one class at a time, so it takes them longer.
A OK, that's good. How much does the program cost?
B Well, let's see. There are six classes, and they're three units each. It's $50 a unit, so that's $900 for the certificate. Books are another $100 per class, and then there's parking and health fees. So the total is about $1,600.
A $1,600? Wow! That's a lot of money.
B Don't worry. There's financial aid for students who qualify.
A OK. You know, I think I'd like to apply. When's the registration deadline?
B Let's see. Looks like it's December fifteenth for the winter semester. You have time.
A But my English, is it good enough?
B Well, you're required to take an English placement test, but I'm sure you'll do fine, Vasili. You're bilingual, you're very motivated, and you have good interpersonal skills. Hospitality and tourism could be a really good career for you.

Page 19, Exercise 3A – Track 11

Vasali hears a radio ad about the Hospitality and Tourism certificate program at La Costa Community College. The ad says graduates can find high-paying jobs in the tourism industry. Vasili goes to see his ESL counselor, Mrs. Ochoa. She tells him about the program requirements, which include an internship in a local tourism business. She also tells him about the deadline for registration, and she says there is financial aid for students who qualify. Vasili is concerned about his English, but Mrs. Ochoa tells him not to worry. Vasili is bilingual, he's very motivated, and he has good interpersonal skills.

Page 24, Exercise 2 – Track 12

An Immigrant Family's Success Story
Choi and Lili Wei left China with their baby boy in the early 1990s. They were poor field workers in their native country, and they wanted their child to have the opportunities they lacked. They arrived in New York and found a one-bedroom apartment in a poor, unstable area. They could only afford a bicycle for transportation, yet they felt fortunate to have the chance to begin a new life in the United States.

Choi and Lili faced many obstacles because they couldn't speak English and had no skills. They found night work cleaning businesses and restaurants. They saved every penny, and after six years, they were able to buy a small restaurant of their own.

They were determined to learn English, get an education, and make a good life for their son. The couple sacrificed a great deal. They never went to the movies, never ate out, and

hardly ever bought anything extra. In their free time, they attended English and citizenship classes. Both of them eventually earned their GED certificates. Choi then enrolled in college while Lili worked in the restaurant.

This past spring, Choi fulfilled a lifelong dream of graduating from college. Now he is registered in a master's degree program in business beginning this fall. And what about their "baby" boy? Their son, Peter, now 21, received a scholarship to a private university, where he is working on his own dream to become an architect.

Choi and Lili are proud to be models of the "American dream." Choi has this advice for other new immigrants: "Find your passion, make a plan to succeed, and don't ever give up."

Unit 3: Friends and family

Page 33, Exercises 2A and 2B – Track 13

Part 1

A You have one new message.
B This call is for Mrs. Wen Lee. This is the attendance office from Central High School calling on Tuesday, March 10th, at 2:00 p.m. We're calling to report an unexcused absence for your daughter, Lan, from her 7th period class today. Please call the office at 619-555-2300 to explain why your daughter missed class. Thank you.

Part 2

C I can't believe we're at the mall on a school day!
D Yeah. Do you think anyone at school is going to miss us?
C No way. There's a substitute teacher in my last period class.
D Mine, too! So, how's everything at home?
C It's the same old thing. I'm so frustrated. My mother won't let me do anything! She is so strict.
D Strict? Like how?
C Well, I'm not permitted to go anywhere without my parents or my brother. And my mom says I can't go out on a date without a chaperone until I'm 18!
D That's so unfair! I wonder why your mother's so strict.
C I don't know. I think she's trying to bring me up like she was raised in China. She just doesn't understand the customs here in the United States.

Part 3

C Hi, Mom.
E Hi, Lan. How was school today?
C Um, fine. Is something wrong?
E The school called and said you were absent from your 7th period class. Where did you go?
C Come on, Mom. Don't get excited.
E Tell me where you went!
C Mary and I just went to the mall right across the street from school, OK?

E But what about your last class?
C There was a substitute teacher, OK? I didn't miss anything!
E I don't understand how you could do this!
C Well, it's your fault! You're so strict that I had no choice. Everybody's allowed to go to the mall except for me. Why can't you trust me?
E This is not about trust. You broke the school rules. You're grounded for the next two weekends.
C Grounded?! What about Celia's birthday party next Saturday?
E I'm afraid you'll have to miss it. Next time, maybe you'll think before you act.

Page 33, Exercise 3A – Track 14

Mrs. Lee received a phone message from her daughter's school saying Lan missed her 7th period class. Lan left school early to go to the mall with her friend Mary. At the mall, Lan tells Mary that her mother is too strict. Lan thinks it's because her mother wants to bring her up the same way she was raised in China. That's why Lan needs a chaperone to go out on a date. At home, Lan and her mother have an argument. Lan is angry because she's not permitted to go to the mall alone. She thinks her mother doesn't trust her. Mrs. Lee is upset because Lan broke the rules. As a punishment, she says Lan is grounded for two weeks.

Page 38, Exercise 2 – Track 15

Barriers Between Generations
In immigrant families, language differences and work schedules often create barriers to communication between the generations. Dolores Suarez, 42, and her son, Diego, 16, face both kinds of barriers every day. Dolores is an immigrant from Mexico who works seven days a week as a housekeeper in a big hotel. She doesn't use much English in her job, and she has never had time to study it. Consequently, her English is limited. Her son, on the other hand, was raised in the United States. He understands Spanish, but he prefers to speak English. When his friends come over to visit, they speak only English. "They talk so fast, I can't understand what they are saying," says Dolores. To make the situation more complicated, Diego and Dolores live with Dolores's father, who speaks Nahuatl, a native language spoken in Mexico. Diego can't understand anything his grandfather says.

Dolores's work schedule is the second barrier to communication with Diego. Because she rarely has a day off, Dolores isn't able to spend much time with him. She doesn't have time to help him with his homework or attend parent-teacher conferences at his school. In 1995, when Dolores immigrated to the United States, her goal was to bring up her son with enough money to avoid the hardships her family suffered in Mexico. Her hard work has permitted Diego to have a comfortable life and a good education.

But she has paid a price for this success. "Sometimes I feel like I don't know my own son," she says.

Unit 4: Health

Page 45, Exercises 2A and 2B – Track 16

Part 1
A Cindy, have you see Sara?
B No. I don't think she's here yet.
A She should have been here 25 minutes ago. Did she call to say she'd be late?
B No, she didn't.
C Oh! Uh, good morning, Mr. Stanley.
A Good morning, Sara.
C I'm sorry, I know I'm late, but the buses are so unreliable.
A I don't know about the buses, Sara, but I do know that if you're late one more time, I'm going to have to fire you.

Part 2
C Thanks for picking me up, Mike.
D No problem.
C We have to hurry – my driving test is in half an hour.
D We have plenty of time. The DMV is just ten minutes from here.
C All right.
D Are you OK? You seem tense.
C Yeah, I'm pretty stressed out.
D How come?
C I was late to work again this morning . . .
D Oh, no!
C And the boss said that if it happens again, he's going to fire me.
D No wonder you're stressed out.
C I'm so worried about losing my job, I can't sleep, I can't eat, I can't concentrate . . .
D You know, Sara, if you're not feeling well, you don't have to take the driving test today.
C Yes, I do, Mike. I have to pass this driving test so I can get my license and buy a car and stop depending on buses.
D OK, OK, I understand. But if you want to pass the test, then you have to calm down. Try to relax. Take a few deep breaths.
C OK.
D Now think positive thoughts. Tell yourself, "I'm a good driver. I'm going to pass my driving test."
C "I'm a good driver, I'm going to pass my driving test."
D Seriously, Sara. You ought to learn some techniques for coping with anxiety.
C Like what?
D Simple stuff. Like I said, deep breathing is good, um, thinking positive thoughts. And I find that it helps me to meditate every day.
C Meditation. Let's talk about it later. Here's the DMV.
D Good luck, and don't forget: You're a good driver!
C Thanks, Mike. You're a good friend.

Page 45, Exercise 3A – Track 17

Mike is driving Sara to the Department of Motor Vehicles (DMV) to take her driving test. He notices that she's very tense. Sara says she's stressed out because she was late to work again. She's worried that her boss will fire her if she's late one more time. She's so afraid of losing her job that she can't eat, she can't sleep, and she can't concentrate. Mike says that she has to calm down if she wants to pass her driving test. He suggests three techniques to help her cope with her anxiety. One is deep breathing. The second one is thinking positive thoughts, and the third one is meditation.

Page 50, Exercise 2 – Track 18

Stress: What You Ought to Know
What is stress?
Stress is our reaction to changing events in our lives. The reactions can be mental – what we think or feel about the changes – and physical – how our body reacts to the changes.
What causes stress?
Stress often comes when there are too many changes in our lives. The changes can be positive, like having a baby or getting a better job, or they can be negative, such as an illness or a divorce. Some stress is healthy. It motivates us to push forward. But too much stress over time can make us sick.
What are the signs of stress?
There are both physical and emotional signs of stress. Physical signs may include tight muscles, elevated blood pressure, grinding your teeth, trouble sleeping, an upset stomach, and back pain. Common emotional symptoms are anxiety, nervousness, depression, trouble concentrating, and nightmares.
How can you manage stress?
To prevent stress, you should eat right and exercise regularly. When you know there will be a stressful event in your day – such as a test, a business meeting, or an encounter with someone you don't get along with – it is really important to eat a healthy breakfast and to limit coffee and sugar.

When you find yourself in a stressful situation, stay calm. Take a few deep breaths to help you relax. Roll your shoulders or stretch to loosen any tight muscles. And take time to think before you speak. You don't want to say something you will regret later!

Unit 5: Around town

Page 59, Exercises 2A and 2B – Track 19

A Hi! Are you the volunteer coordinator?
B Yup, Steve Jones. And you're Almaz? Did I say it right?
A Yes, exactly, Almaz Bekele. Nice to meet you.
B You, too. Please have a seat. I was just looking over your application to volunteer here at Quiet Palms, and

it looks really good. Is it OK if I ask you some questions?

A Of course. Go ahead.

B OK, let's see. You wrote that you've been a volunteer before. Can you tell me about that?

A Sure. I volunteered last summer at the public library downtown.

B What did you do there?

A I worked with adults who wanted to learn how to read. I also taught a little writing, and on Saturdays, I read stories to the kids.

B Did you enjoy that?

A Yeah, but what I really liked was working with the older people. It felt like I was doing something really worthwhile.

B Uh-huh. So now tell me why you want to volunteer in a nursing home.

A Well, I think I might want to work in the health-care field someday, but I won't know for sure until I get some experience.

B I see. Well, we'd love to have you volunteer here.

A Great! When can I start?

B I like your enthusiasm, but we have some health requirements. First, you need to take a blood test and a TB test. You can start as soon as we get the results. It usually takes two or three days.

A OK. I'll take care of that right away. Also, um, I was wondering – can you tell me what my responsibilities will be?

B Sure. One thing volunteers do is, uh, they help residents with their meals. You might encourage them to eat, or just keep them company during mealtime.

A Yeah, my grandmother always eats more when I'm with her. She likes having people around.

B Then I'm sure you understand that you need to be patient and compassionate with the residents.

A I know.

B Volunteers also deliver mail and flowers, and they take residents for walks. You'll get more responsibilities as soon as you feel more confident.

A Sounds good.

B There's an orientation next Monday at 8:30.

A I'll be there!

B One more thing. You'll need to make a commitment to volunteer at least three hours per week.

A No problem! I can't wait to start.

Page 59, Exercise 3A – Track 20

Last summer, Almaz volunteered at the public library downtown. She liked working with the older people because she felt that she was doing something worthwhile. Today, she is meeting with Steve, the volunteer coordinator at Quiet Palms, a nursing home. She wants to volunteer there to find out if she likes working in the health-care field. Steve tells her about some of her responsibilities at Quiet Palms. He says it's very important for volunteers to be compassionate and patient when they are working with the residents. He asks Almaz to make a commitment to volunteer at least three hours per week. Almaz agrees to attend an orientation. She says she can't wait to start volunteering.

Page 64, Exercise 2 – Track 21

Running with Ropes

Imagine running with your eyes closed. How do you feel? Insecure? Afraid? Justin Andrews knows these feelings very well. Justin is a former long-distance runner who lost his vision because of a grave illness. For the past six months, he has been running twice a week with the help of volunteer runners at Running with Ropes, an organization that assists blind and visually impaired runners. "Running with Ropes has changed my life," Justin says. "Until I heard about it, I thought I'd never run outside again."

Volunteers at Running with Ropes make a commitment to volunteer two to four hours a week. Scott Liponi, one of the running volunteers, explains what they do. "We use ropes to join ourselves to the blind runners and guide them around and over obstacles, such as holes in the road and other runners." Scott has learned how to keep the rope loose so the blind runner has more freedom. He deeply respects the blind runners' tenacity. "They are incredibly determined," he says. "It doesn't matter if it's hot, raining, or snowing – they are going to run." Scott says it is gratifying to share in the joy of the runners and to feel that they trust him. "The four hours I spend at Running with Ropes are the most rewarding part of my week," he says. "It's really a worthwhile commitment."

Unit 6: Time

Page 71, Exercises 2A and 2B – Track 22

Part 1

A Excuse me, ma'am?

B Yes?

A I'm a reporter for KESL Radio, and today we're asking people for their opinions about technology and time-saving devices. Do you have a minute to answer some questions for me?

B Sure.

A May I have your name?

B Jean Rosen. Mrs. Rosen.

A Do you have a favorite time-saving device?

B Let me see. . . . I guess it's this – my address stamper.

A Oh. I expected something electronic, not manual! Does it really save you time?

B Absolutely. It takes about a minute to handwrite a return address. The address stamper just takes seconds, even though it's not electronic.

A Thank you for your time, Mrs. Rosen.

Part 2

A Excuse me, sir. Do you have a minute?

C Well, I'm in a bit of a hurry.

A I'm a reporter for KESL Radio. I'm asking people for their opinions about how technology helps them save time.

C Technology – a time-saver? I'm afraid you're talking to the wrong man. I'm not a fan of technology.

A Why is that?

C Well, take e-mail, for example. Half the time it's spam. And it's distracting, too. It interrupts my work.

A But isn't it convenient?

C Not that I can see. If you ask me, most of this electronic stuff wastes more time than it saves. I still write letters by hand although I have a perfectly good computer at home.

A I see. Could I get your name before you go?

C Ronald Chung.

A Thank you for your time, Mr. Chung.

Part 3

A Good morning, ma'am. I'm a reporter for KESL Radio.

D Yes?

A I'm asking people their opinions about technology and time-saving devices.

D Oh, that sounds interesting.

A Do you have a favorite time-saving device?

D Oh, yes. I just love my cell phone.

A I guess it saves you lots of time because you can use it anywhere.

D That's right. You see, I go to lots of sales to buy clothes for my daughter. I take pictures with my camera phone of clothes I think she might like.

A Really?

D Yeah. Then I send her the pictures while I'm still in the store. She sends me a text message back. It says "Buy" or "Don't buy."

A Now that's innovative.

D Yeah. Not a bad idea, huh?

A I'm sure our listeners will enjoy hearing about such an unusual use.

D Happy to share. It really is a time-saver. But not a money-saver.

A I see what you mean! Oh, I didn't get your name.

D Patricia Morales.

A Well, thank you, Ms. Morales, for sharing your favorite time-saving device.

Page 71, Exercise 3A – Track 23

Today, a reporter from KESL Radio asked three people about technology and their favorite time-saving devices. Mrs. Rosen's favorite device is manual. She says it saves time, even though it isn't electronic. Mr. Chung isn't a fan of technology. In fact, he says technology wastes more time than it saves. For example, he says he doesn't like e-mail because he gets lots of spam. He also finds e-mail distracting. He doesn't think it is convenient. Ms. Morales loves technology. She uses the camera on her cell phone in a very innovative way – to send her daughter pictures of clothes that are on sale. Her daughter sends a text message back: "Buy" or "Don't buy."

Page 76, Exercise 2 – Track 24

The Impact of Technology
By Katelyn Houston

Changes in technology can change people's lives.

When my great-grandmother was born in 1900, her family lived on a ranch, and they went to town in a horse and buggy. Cars were rare; people thought they were dangerous pieces of machinery. By the time my great-grandmother died in 1979, nearly everyone owned a car, and horse buggies were in museums.

Although transportation technology has not changed significantly in my own lifetime, there have been huge changes in the way we get the news. Newspapers were once people's primary source for the news: in 1965, 72 percent of Americans reported that they read a newspaper on an average day. By 2005, that number was down to 50 percent. Today hardly anyone reads the newspaper! Another common way that people got news in the past was by listening to the radio, which began to broadcast news in the 1920s. I suppose nearly everyone had a radio then. However, by the 1950s, television was overtaking radio. Now even the number of people watching the news on television has declined, dropping from 60 percent in 1993 to 28 percent in 2006. So what's the latest source for news? The Web. The number of Americans who use the Internet to get the news is increasing. Most people access the news on their smart phones.

Yet another example of change is how we pay for goods and services. Until the mid-1940s, people had to carry large amounts of cash in their purses and wallets. Then, one day in 1949, when a man named Frank McNamara took some business associates to dinner, he left his wallet at home. He had to call his wife to bring him money to pay the bill. I think it was probably the most embarrassing moment of his life!

Mr. McNamara vowed to find a way to avoid carrying cash. Some stores already had their own charge cards, but there was no single, multi-purpose credit card. A year later he returned to the same restaurant with the same people, but paid with the credit card he had created, called "Diner's Club." A year after that second dinner, 42,000 people in the United States had the card, and two years after that, the card was also used in Canada, Cuba, Mexico, and the United Kingdom. I bet that paying with plastic will soon be as antiquated as the horse and buggy. Already, many people pay for things with their smart phones.

In what other ways to do you think technology may change our lives in the future?

Unit 7: Shopping

Page 85, Exercises 2A and 2B – Track 25

Part 1

A Excuse me. Do you work here?
B Yes. Do you need some help?
A Where do I take this thing?
B What have you got there?
A It's a camera, a digital camera. I'd like to get my money back, if possible.
B OK, if you want a refund, you need to talk to somebody in Customer Service. See that guy who's wearing a red tie over there? He'll help you.
A Thank you.

Part 2

C Who's next?
A Hi. I want to return this camera that I bought. I'd like to get my money back.
C You bought it here? Do you have the receipt?
A The receipt? Just a minute. Here it is.
C OK. That's good. Is the camera defective?
A What do you mean – "defective"?
C Well, is there something wrong with it? Doesn't it work?
A Oh, no – it's not broken or anything. I just don't like it.
C What's the problem?
A It's the screen.
C The screen?
A Yeah. The screen is too small. A few days ago, I was taking pictures. It was a sunny day, and I couldn't see the picture in the screen! Maybe it's my eyes.
C No, I don't think it's your eyes. That screen is kind of small. So, did you want to exchange it for another camera?
A I'm not sure. Is it possible to get my money back?
C Well, let me look at that receipt again. You got this on the 5th, and today is the 20th. So it's been 15 days. Our policy for a refund is that you have to bring it back within 10 days. So, sorry – no refund.
A Oh. I didn't know about the 10 days.
C Now, for an exchange: You have 30 days – if the merchandise is in perfect condition.
A Oh, it's just like new! I only used it a couple of times. Here, see for yourself.
C Yeah, you're right. Looks OK to me. Is everything in the box?
A I think so. Like I said, I hardly used the camera. Here's the case that came with it. And here's the instruction book, and the warranty card, and all the papers that –
C OK, great. Why don't I keep this camera here while you look around the store?
A You mean, I have to choose another camera today? I'm kind of in a hurry.

C Well, if you want, I could just give you a store credit instead. With a store credit, you can come back and shop anytime.
A Oh, that's a good idea. Maybe I can bring my nephew with me next time I come. He knows a lot about cameras.
C OK, let me get you a store credit.
A I really appreciate all your help.
C No problem.

Page 85, Exercise 3A – Track 26

Rosa wants to return the camera that she bought and get a refund. She is told that she needs to speak with someone in customer service. The clerk there asks Rosa if the camera is defective, and she says it isn't. The clerk tells her about the store policy for returns and exchanges. It's too late for Rosa to return the camera, but she can exchange it if the merchandise is in perfect condition. Rosa still has the camera box with the instruction book and the warranty card. Since Rosa is in a hurry, she decides to get a store credit, and she will use it at a later time.

Page 90, Exercise 2 – Track 27

The Smart Shopper
Dear smart shopper,

I'm a jewelry lover, and I enjoy shopping online. Unfortunately, I just bought a pair of gold earrings that I don't like. When I tried to return them, I learned that the seller has a no-return policy. Don't I have the right to get a refund?
– Mad Madelyn

Dear Mad Madelyn,

If the merchandise is defective, the seller must return your money or make an exchange. However, if the merchandise was in good condition when you received it, and if the retailer has a no-return policy, there is nothing you can do. This is true for store purchases as well as Internet purchases. In the future, here are some questions you should ask before you buy anything:

• Does the seller say "satisfaction guaranteed or your money back"?
• Is there a time limit on returns, such as two weeks?
• Who pays the shipping costs on items that are returned?
• Do you need to return the merchandise in its original package?
• Is the original receipt required?
• Does the retailer give a store credit instead of a cash refund?
• If the retailer has a store in your area, can you return the merchandise to the store instead of shipping it?

Next time, find the return policy on the merchant's Web site and print it, or ask the merchant for the return policy in writing. It's important to get all the facts that you need before you buy!
–Smart Shopper

Unit 8: Work

Page 97, Exercises 2A and 2B – Track 28

Part 1

A David, can I talk to you for a second?
B Yeah, sure.
A Um, you know, you've been leaving early a lot lately, and when you do that, I have to stay later and close up the shop by myself.
B Oh, come on, Yolanda. That doesn't happen very often.
A Well, it happened twice last week, and it's happened once so far this week. I'd say that's pretty often. Plus, sometimes the shop is full of customers, and you're in the back room talking on your cell phone. So I feel like I've been doing my job and yours, too. It's not fair. Something's wrong here. We have to figure out a better system here so we divide the work more equally.
B OK, whatever – but I have to go now. See you!

Part 2

C Yolanda, over here!
A Hi, guys.
D Whoa, Yolanda – what's wrong?
A I'm exhausted. I've just finished work.
D Don't you usually finish at 4:00?
A Yeah, Teresa, but the other guy on my shift, David, he's going to night school, and lately he's been leaving early a lot. So then I have to clean up the shop and close up by myself. Sometimes I don't get out of there until 4:45 or 5:00. It's really frustrating.
D That's really unfair.
C I think you should quit that job!
D Quit? That's crazy, Julie. She can't quit – it's hard to find another job!
C Well, have you tried talking to David?
A Yeah, I talked to him, but it didn't help.
D What about your boss? Have you told her?
A No, not yet. I'd really like to try to work something out with David first.
C Listen, I have an idea. What about making a chart?
A A chart? How does that work?
C It's simple. You make a list of all the duties in your shift. You know – open up, make coffee, whatever. Then you negotiate with David and decide who's going to do which tasks.
A OK . . .
C And then, every day, as soon as you finish a task, you write your initials on the chart.
A I get it. So then if David isn't doing his share, it's easy to see.
C And if the problem continues, you can show the chart to your boss and let her deal with it.
A I like that idea, Julie. Especially the part about negotiating with David. I really hope we can work this out together.

Page 97, Exercise 3A – Track 29

Yolanda and David work at Daria's Donut Shop. Lately, David has been leaving work early, and Yolanda has to close up the shop by herself. Tonight, Yolanda is having coffee with her friends. She is exhausted. Her friends give her advice. Teresa thinks she should talk to her boss, but Yolanda wants to try to work things out with David first. Julie thinks Yolanda should make a chart of their duties. Then she should negotiate with David and decide who is going to do which tasks. When they finish a task, they should write their initials on the chart. If David isn't doing his share of the work, it will show in the chart. Then Yolanda can show the chart to their boss and let her deal with the situation.

Page 102, Exercise 2 – Track 30

Hard and Soft Job Skills

Som Sarawong has been working as an automotive technician at George's Auto Repair for over five years. Today was a special day for Som, a 35-year-old Thai immigrant, because he received the Employee of the Year award. According to Ed Overton, Som's boss, Som received the award "because he's a great 'people person' and he has superb technical skills. I even have him work on my own car!"

Som has the two kinds of skills that are necessary to be successful and move up in his career: soft skills and hard skills. Soft skills are personal and social skills. Som gets along with his co-workers. He has a strong work ethic; in five years, he has never been late or absent from work. Customers trust him. Hard skills, on the other hand, are the technical skills a person needs to do a job. Som can repair cars, trucks, and motorcycles. He learned from his father, who was also a mechanic. Then he took classes and got a certificate as an auto technician.

Soft and hard skills are equally important, but hard skills are easier to teach and assess than soft skills. People can learn how to use a machine and then take a test on their knowledge. However, it's harder to teach people how to be cooperative and have a good work ethic. George Griffith, the owner of George's Auto Repair, explains, "I've been working in this business for over 30 years, and most of the time when I've needed to fire someone, it was because of weak people skills, not because they didn't have technical abilities." Soft skills and good technical knowledge are a winning combination, and today, Som Sarawong was the winner.

Unit 9: Daily living

Page 111, Exercises 2A and 2B – Track 31

A Mei! Dinner!
B I'll be right there! Sorry I'm late. I was just checking something on the computer.

A OK. Sit down. We've been waiting for you.
B I know. I'm sorry, but I was looking at the Web site for this great organization called the Living Green Council.
C "Living green"? What does that mean? I don't even like that color.
B Dad, it means taking responsibility for saving the earth.
C Saving it from what?
B From global warming! We had a guest speaker today in biology class, and he mentioned a whole bunch of stuff – simple steps we can take to reduce our energy use and protect the environment.
A Like what?
B OK, well, first of all, he said we need to cut down on driving, so we should walk, ride a bicycle, carpool, or take public transportation.
C I'd do those things if I could. But my job is an hour away, and there's no bus service that goes there. And there's nobody for me to carpool with.
B I see your point, but how about recycling? I think we could do a better job of recycling bottles, cans, glass, paper . . .
A You're right. We could do that if we tried.
B Another idea was to turn off unnecessary lights. Look at this house: lights on in every room.
C I like that idea. It'll help cut down on the electric bill.
A What else did the speaker suggest?
B Let me think. Oh, he said that we should wash our clothes in cold water.
A Really? I'm not sure the clothes will get clean, but I suppose we can try.
C That'll save money on the electric bill, too.
B But isn't our washing machine really old? If we bought a new one that's more energy-efficient, it could help the environment and our electric bill!
A I don't think we can afford to buy new appliances right now.
B OK. But what about energy-efficient lightbulbs? We could switch to those, right?
A That sounds pretty simple, Mei.
B Cool!
C I have to say, I love your enthusiasm. I never realized how simple it can be to . . . what did you call it . . . "live green"?
B Yeah, the speaker said that if everyone did even one of these things every day, it would do a lot to reduce global warming.
C Speaking of warming, can we eat before the food gets cold?

Page 111, Exercise 3A – Track 32

Mei was late to dinner because she was looking at the Web site of the Living Green Council. "Living green" means taking responsibility for saving the earth from global warming. Mei tells her parents about the guest speaker who came to her class. The speaker suggested simple things people could do to reduce their energy use and protect the environment. For example, they could carpool instead of driving alone, recycle their bottles and cans, and use energy-efficient lightbulbs. Mei's parents agree that it is important to cut down on energy use since it would also help them save money. However, they can't afford to buy new appliances right now.

Page 116, Exercise 2 – Track 33

All Things Are Connected

Long ago, there was a village chief who never allowed anyone to disagree with him. Whenever he wanted to do something, he asked the members of his court for their advice. But whether the chief's idea was wise or foolish, his advisors always said the same thing: "Indeed, it is wise." Only one old woman dared to give a different answer. Whenever the chief asked for her advice, she always replied, "All things are connected."

One night, the chief was awakened by the sound of frogs croaking in the swamp. It happened again the next night and the next and the next. The chief decided to kill all the frogs in the swamp. When he consulted the members of his court, they replied as usual: "Indeed, it is wise." But the old woman kept silent. "And you, old woman, what do you think?" the chief demanded. "All things are connected," she replied. The chief concluded that the old woman was a fool, and he ordered his servants to kill all the frogs. Therefore, the chief slept peacefully.

But soon the mosquitoes in the swamp began to multiply since there were no frogs to eat them. They came into the village and made everyone miserable. The chief ordered his servants to go into the swamp and kill the mosquitoes, but it was impossible. Furious, the chief summoned the members of his court and blamed them, saying, "Why didn't you tell me that killing the frogs would make the mosquitoes multiply and everyone would be miserable? I should have listened to the old woman."

Because the mosquitoes were there, all the people of the village were forced to go away. Finally, the chief and his family left, too. Until he died the chief never forgot the old woman's words: "All things are connected."

Unit 10: Free time

Page 123, Exercises 2A and 2B – Track 34

A Hi, Cathy. What are you doing this weekend?

B Oh, Thanh. I'm glad you asked. I was invited to Bao and An's wedding. It's Saturday night, and I haven't bought them a gift yet.

A So?

B Well, I don't know what to get them. They aren't registered at any stores.

A Registered? What's that?

B Well, for many American weddings, the bride and groom sign up with a gift registry service at a store. They make a list of what they want, and then people can go to the store or the store's Web site and buy something on the couple's list.

A I've never heard of that custom. At a Vietnamese wedding, guests just bring cash in an envelope.

B Really?

A Yeah, and during the reception, the bride and groom walk from table to table, greet the guests, and collect the envelopes. If I were you, I would just take an envelope.

B OK. Thanks for the advice. I guess customs are really different across cultures, aren't they?

A That's for sure. Do you know what really surprised me the first time I went to an American wedding?

B No, what?

A As the bride and groom were leaving the reception, the guests threw rice at them. What a waste of food! Where does that custom come from?

B Oh, that's a really old tradition. Rice is a symbol of fertility and longevity, so throwing rice represents the hope that the couple will have children and live a long life together.

A That's really interesting.

B Yeah. So, Thanh, what else happens at a Vietnamese wedding?

A Well, for one thing, it's traditional for a Vietnamese bride to wear a red dress.

B Red? Not white, like in this country?

A That's right. In our culture, red symbolizes good fortune. In fact, one of the traditional foods at a Vietnamese wedding is red sticky rice.

B Interesting. Let me ask you something else. My invitation was just for the wedding reception in the evening. What about the ceremony?

A Well, traditionally, the ceremony takes place at the bride's home, with just the family and close relatives. It's usually held in the morning. The reception in the evening is actually a huge party, with all the couple's friends and acquaintances, lots of dancing, and lots of food. Be prepared for a seven- or eight-course dinner.

B Wow! I guess I won't eat anything beforehand. So, will I see you at Bao and An's wedding?

A I wish I could go, but I have to go to my nephew's graduation party. I hope you have a great time.

B I hope so, too. I'm really looking forward to it.

Page 123, Exercise 3A – Track 35

Cathy and Thanh are talking about wedding customs. Cathy is invited to a Vietnamese wedding, and she is surprised that the bride and groom are not registered for gifts at any stores. In contrast, Thanh is surprised by the American tradition of throwing rice at the bride and groom. Next, they talk about clothes. Thanh says a Vietnamese bride wears a red dress because the color red symbolizes good fortune. Then Cathy asks why she was invited only to the wedding reception, not the ceremony. Thanh explains that traditionally the ceremony is only for the family. The couple's friends and acquaintances are invited to the evening reception. In fact, Thanh says the evening party will include seven or eight courses of food. Cathy says she is looking forward to the wedding.

Page 128, Exercise 2 – Track 36

Special Birthdays Around the World

In most cultures, there are certain birthdays that are especially important in a young person's life. If you were an American teenager, for example, you would eagerly look forward to your 16th birthday because in most states, that is the age to get a driver's license. Other cultures also have birthdays with special meanings:

Mexico For Mexican girls, the 15th birthday – the "Quinceañera" – symbolizes a girl's transition into adulthood. To celebrate, the girl's family throws a huge party. The girl wears a ball gown similar to a wedding dress. The girl performs a waltz, a formal dance, with her father. A similar custom is celebrated in Brazil.

China On a child's first birthday, parents place their baby in the center of a group of objects, such as a shiny coin, a book, and a doll. Then they watch to see which object the baby picks up first. Most parents hope their child will pick up the coin because, according to tradition, it means the child will be rich.

Nigeria The 1st, 5th, 10th, and 15th birthdays are considered extremely important. Parties are held with up to 100 people. The guests enjoy a feast of a roasted cow or goat.

Saudi Arabia In some countries, such as Saudi Arabia, people don't observe birthdays at all because of spiritual beliefs. According to Muslim traditions, the only celebrations allowed are Eid al Fitr, a feast that signifies the end of Ramadan, and Eid al Adha, which celebrates the end of the annual pilgrimage to Mecca.

Israel A boy's 13th and a girl's 12th birthdays are serious as well as happy occasions. On these birthdays, children become responsible for their own religious and moral behavior.

Adult birthdays also have special significance in many cultures. In the United States, for example, birthdays ending in "0" – 30, 40, 50, etc. – are especially meaningful.

Illustration credits

Kenneth Batelman: 73
Adrian D'Alimonte: 12, 16
Nina Edwards: 37, 46, 89
Chuck Gonzales: 49, 66, 74, 116

Brad Hamann: 64, 87
Q2A Media Services: 2, 11, 69, 76, 107, 121, 122 (t)
Monika Roe: 61, 101, 113

Photography credits